The Essence of Operations Management

Terry Hill
London Business School

Prentice Hall
New York   London   Toronto   Sydney   Tokyo   Singapore

First published 1993 by
Prentice Hall International (UK) Ltd
Campus 400, Maylands Avenue
Hemel Hempstead
Hertfordshire, HP2 7EZ
A division of
Simon & Schuster International Group

Typeset in 10/12pt Palatino by
Keyset Composition, Colchester
Printed and bound in Great Britain by
BPC Wheatons Ltd, Exeter

Library of Congress Cataloging-in-Publication Data

Hill, Terry, 1940–
    The essence of operations management/Terry Hill.
    p. cm. – (The Essence of management series)
    Includes bibliographical references and index.
    ISBN 0-13-284845-7
    1. Industrial management.   I. Title.   II. Series.
HD31.H4897   1993
658–dc20   92-38466
                                                          CIP

British Library Cataloguing in Publication Data

A catalogue record for this book is available from the British
Library

ISBN 0-13-284845-7 (pbk)

---

3 4 5   96 95

To
PM, AJ and JB

Contents

1

Managing operations

The 1980s proved to be more challenging and difficult for the operations manager than any other time since the Industrial Revolution. The 1990s will prove even more so. The traditional problems of out-of-date technologies, underdeveloped infrastructures, inefficient work methods and manning arrangements, inappropriate payment systems and ineffective scheduling and control systems have been coupled with a whole set of new challenges – increasing world competition, decreasing product/service life cycles, customers' expectations regarding quality and product performance, stringent regulations concerning employees, the environment and safety protection, together with the scarcity and rising costs of energy and raw materials. Furthermore, the linked world economy has resulted in a more complex business environment, with new and different competitive situations bound up with legal and tax issues and the different political, social and business pressures which exist – a situation, the difficulties of which have been accelerated by the forming and breakdown of political blocs and the subsequent market opportunities which have resulted.

Similar pressures have started to unfold in the service sector. Although many service industries are protected to varying degrees by geography, many major services have increasingly been subjected to national and international competition. This move from sheltered to traded environments within the service sector is continuing. Deregulation in US airlines, the growth in the hotel chain concept and the interrelation between share and money markets through the world's stock and financial centres have imposed similar demands on related businesses and highlighted the

1

importance of the operations manager's role. Although the phenomenon of international (and for some services even national) competition will·be less widespread than in the manufacturing sector, it will show similar increases, if not at the same overall level. The continued and significant improvements in data storage and transmission will open up many areas to competition and spawn services new in themselves or in their application.

As a consequence, the operations manager will need increasingly to provide the support essential to the success of the wide range of goods and services involved, different in themselves, and changing in nature over time with life cycles which will continue to become shorter. New efforts to increase productivity, to create technological advantage and to find additional methods to increase the return on assets will be part of the challenge facing those in charge of these functions.

The role of operations management

Production management and operations management describe the same set of tasks. Both are concerned with managing those resources of an enterprise that are required to produce the goods or services to be sold to consumers or other organizations. The term 'production management' came first, with the emergence of manufacturing industry and the subsequent emphasis placed on the production management task within that sector. The growth of service industries in the industrially developed countries has brought with it the term 'operations management' as a more appropriate general title. Throughout this book, therefore, the terms 'production management' and 'operations management' will be treated as synonymous.

The mix of manufactured items and services

As economies develop, the relative mix of the primary, secondary and tertiary sectors changes. For more developed countries, there has been a growing and distinct shift towards the tertiary sector and away from the primary and secondary sectors, as shown in Table 1.1.

Table 1.1 Percentage of gross domestic product by sector[a] grouping for certain more developed economies (1989)

Country	Primary	Secondary	Tertiary
Australia	8	24	68
Belgium	2	27	71
Canada*	10	25	65
Denmark	5	22	73
France	8	27	69
Japan	3	38	59
Netherlands	7	26	67
UK*	8	28	64
USA*	7	27	66
USSR*	21	56	24
W. Germany*	2	38	60

[a]These sectors include the following activities:
primary – agriculture and mining;
secondary – manufacturing and construction;
tertiary – utilities, wholesale/retail trade, transport, services and others (unclassified activities which constitute in all instances a relatively high percentage of the total GDP).
*Figures are for 1987.
Source: UN Bulletin of Statistics (July 1991).

However, it is important to remember that most organizations provide and sell a mixed products/services offering. This will change from market to market and between segments within a market, as shown in Figure 1.1.

What characterizes all of these, however, is the role of the operations function. The provision of a service or production of a product will be the principal responsibility of operations and will entail a number of tasks, the characteristics of which together make up the operations management role. The key features which make up the tasks are now explained.

Managing a large cost centre

The operations function is typically responsible for some 80 per cent of all the costs incurred by a business. These comprise most, if not all, the direct costs (employees and materials) and a portion of the overheads which fall within its jurisdiction.

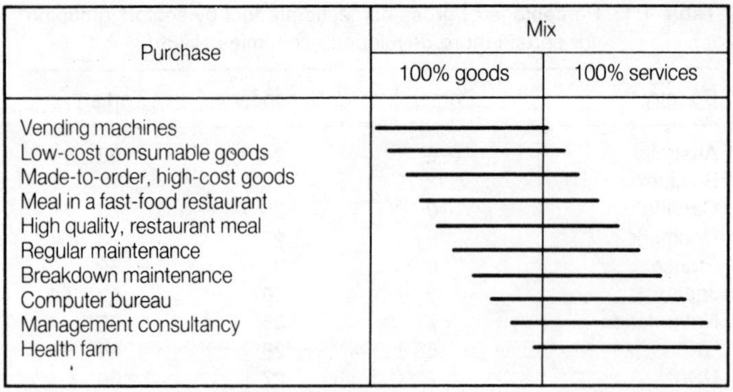

Purchase	Mix	
	100% goods	100% services
Vending machines Low-cost consumable goods Made-to-order, high-cost goods Meal in a fast-food restaurant High quality, restaurant meal Regular maintenance Breakdown maintenance Computer bureau Management consultancy Health farm		

Source: Terry Hill, *Production/Operations Management: Text and cases* (2nd edn), Prentice Hall International, Hemel Hempstead, 1991, p. 7 (with permission).

Figure 1.1 Different product/service mixes provided in a range of purchases

Managing the work and money flow

The basic task in operations is to take inputs in the form of resources and convert them into outputs in the form of products and services. This conversion process (see Figure 1.2), therefore, is at the core of operations and comprises the basic workflow throughout an organization.

However, given the high level of costs involved, the function also has a prime role in managing the money flow. This comes simply from the fact that costs are built up as a product/service moves from raw materials through work-in-progress to finished goods. The purchase of raw materials, components and subassemblies and the direct labour costs involved in the conversion process need, therefore, to be well managed and controlled as they reflect key elements of cash flow. Thus, within operations rests a substantial portion of two key elements of a successful business – profits through the control of costs, and cash flow through planning decisions and lead-time control.

Interface between the doing and thinking ends of a business

The operations function provides the essential interface between corporate direction and the operational task, and the corporate

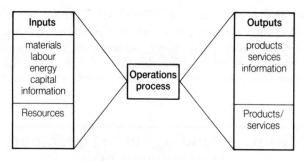

Source: Hill, op. cit., p. 4 (with permission).

Figure 1.2 Outline of the operations process

philosophies and individual value systems which reside within an organization.

Measurement by tangible outputs

Unlike most functions, the performance within operations can be measured in tangible terms. Whilst this offers many advantages, it also normally leads to reinforcing of detailed, short-term reviews with correspondingly less emphasis on the long term, a fact which will be discussed more fully in Chapter 2.

Managing the short and long term

As implied in the last point, executives need to manage the short and long term well within the frame of the operations function. Given the large cost, asset and people base referred to earlier, managing costs within set and agreed budgets is essential to the short-term prosperity of a business. In the same way, the large cost, asset and people base within operations offers saving opportunities of a substantial nature.

Managing complexity

The descriptions of the operations management task given so far have underlined the dimensions of size and importance. One outcome of these characteristics concerns the issue of managing complexity. However, this is not to say that the individual facets of the task are complex; they are no more so than the elements of most managers' jobs. What creates the complexity is the interrelationship between the many dimensions which comprise the operations task. The number of facets is a direct outcome of the function's size (assets, costs and people) whilst the interrelationship is due to the linked nature of all these elements within the function itself.

Misunderstandings of the operations management task

Having described the key features and elements of the operations management task it will be beneficial to clarify further the nature of this key managerial and functional role by highlighting two specific areas of misunderstanding. These concern production engineering and operations research.

Production engineering

Within a manufacturing company, production engineering is often confused with production management. However, a review of any firm will illustrate the different sets of functional responsibilities and tasks which go with the two jobs. Invariably they have different reporting structures. The reason for this is fundamental to the sets of responsibilities involved. Whereas production management is concerned with the conversion process and with the distinct features and tasks which go with that, production engineering is a staff function which provides specialist support in the areas of equipment/processes technologies and associated areas of expertise.

The misunderstanding which exists between these functions emanates to some extent from the perception of the role, importance and integral nature of technology and engineering in manufacturing. But operations is not a technical/engineering-related function but a business-related function. The only exception is in firms which provide one-off specialist products or services. In these low-volume situations, the operations manager will be involved in both the product/service specification and alignment of capability (processes and people) with the tasks to be completed. However, these business situations are the exception rather than the rule, as more fully explained in Chapter 4. Most businesses make standard products using known processes with specialist engineering/

technical functions as part of the support provision. Thus, the product/service and process technologies (no matter how involved and sophisticated) are givens. The task of the operations manager is to provide the critical business orientation which this function should provide.

Operations research

The second basic and almost universal misunderstanding comes with the area known as operations (or operational) research (OR). In part, the confusion comes from the word 'operations' and, in part, from the fact that the majority of applications of OR techniques are in the area of operations management.

In the 1960s and 1970s, scholars and business people were optimistic about the future role of OR techniques such as linear programming, model building, computer simulation, dynamic programming and other computer-related applications in organizations. It was implied, if not explicitly argued, that these developments would routinize many of the traditional functions of middle management, typically in the operations functions.

The use of such techniques draws both its origins and argued relevance from the specialist functions which developed these approaches. It is only since the early 1980s, however, that the approaches have been challenged, both in terms of the usefulness of their application in companies and the consequent relevance of their position in the teaching and research activities under the umbrella of operations management.

The change in orientation towards the management of operations has been both timely and relevant, even though late in the day. However, as with many changes, the inertia of the past has been hard to shake off. The residual presence of operations research activity in the form of lingering arguments, past applications and existing resources is still in evidence. Though the confusion with operations management has been clearly identified, reinforcement of the difference needs to be continuously highlighted.

Key points review

The size of operations underscores the need for this function to be managed well, both in the short and long term. The control of some

70–80 per cent of costs is at the core of working to budgeted performances. Continuous improvement in these same large areas will, on the other hand, yield the best potential results. Managing these essential tasks is at the core of the operations task.

However, key developments in the operations function have only more recently attracted the necessary level of resources and have been given appropriate direction. Managing this area as a business function and prioritizing developments and activities in line with market needs have only recently come to the fore, a fact covered in more detail in the next chapter. However, the complexity of the task has often hindered this key and appropriate orientation. But if companies are to succeed in today's markets then the role of operations needs to be at the forefront of a firm's strategic response.

2

Strategic context

Faced with increasing competitive pressures, businesses have a greater need to coordinate the activities of their principal functions within a coherent strategy. However, they often fail to do this. They do not embrace all the functional contributions necessary to develop successful corporate responses. One common and glaring omission is that of the production/operations function.

Functions dominate strategic outcomes

One characteristic which typifies strategic debate is that individual functions dominate corporate strategy outcomes. This, in part, has its origins in history, as Table 2.1 illustrates. The result, however it came to be, is that corporate strategy formulation fails to embrace the dimensions of all key functions and their interrelation one with another.

Functional strategies *vis-à-vis* a corporate strategy

Whilst corporate documents are compiled they are typically no more than the strategic statements of functions prepared individually with

9

Table 2.1 Changes in the dominant role of functions in corporate strategy formulation

Period	Typical function	Reasons
1945 to 1965	Production/ operations	During this period, in most industrial sectors world demand was greater than world capacity. Companies could typically, therefore, sell all they could make and hence the production/ operations function tended to hold sway in strategic debate.
1965 to early 1980s	Marketing	In about the mid-1960s, the imbalance between available world capacity and world demand had begun to be redressed. The outcome was that in most markets selling products became increasingly difficult. Hence the advent of marketing's strategic role which came to the fore from this time onwards.
Early 1980s to present day	Marketing and/or finance	The recession which occurred in the late 1970s and early 1980s resulted in many companies experiencing financial difficulties and witnessed a spate of corporate failures. Already gaining ground, these events stimulated the emergence of the finance/accounting function and its role in strategic formulation.

little or no debate on how these key perspectives interrelate with one another. The need to identify the level of match or mismatch which exists between functional strategies is at the very core of corporate strategy formulation. Only through this interchange can a company reconcile differences, identify implications and assess investments and time-scales. Only in this way can firms arrive at well-thought-through, well-articulated and coordinated corporate strategies which all functions understand, have agreed and will be able to support.

There is an urgent need for companies to review the way in which they develop strategies. The nearest they get to inter-functional debate is that these individually prepared statements sit side by side in the same binder. Charged individually to prepare a functional strategy, each part of the business responds and arrives at its own view of what is best for the business as a whole. The inherent ramifications of one function's strategy on other functions is not discussed. But this interchange is the very essence of strategy formulation. Without it, and given the dynamic nature of today's markets, companies will become increasingly disadvantaged.

The reactive role of operations management

When developing a corporate strategy, many companies have neither the way, nor sometimes the will, to incorporate the necessary functional perspectives essential to determining an appropriate corporate strategy response.

As discussed above and illustrated in Table 2.1, whilst most companies recognize the need to embrace the marketing perspectives and to identify financial constraints, few incorporate the critical perspectives of operations management. Part of the reason why is the historical perspective discussed earlier – the way it has always been done. There are also other reasons, including the following.

The characteristic traits of operations managers – emotional and verbal

The characteristics which typify operations managers are those of being emotional and verbal. Why? In part, this comes from the nature of the operations task. No one expects marketing/sales to sell on one day a fifth of that week's sales, or in one week to sell a quarter of that month's sales, or in a given month to sell a twelfth of that year's sales. But they do need to make or provide in any given hour one hour's worth of that day's scheduled output. The consequence is that to manage operations successfully, those responsible need to handle the short term well and develop a capability to ensure that this happens regularly and repeatedly. This calls for emotional drive and an appropriate emphasis on this capability.

The verbal characteristic describes operations managers' reluctance to explain relevant perspectives using the written word. Instead, their culture is one based on verbal complaint which fails to offer coherent insights into the strategic origins of why problems have arisen. With data all around them, operations managers fail to collect and review systematically the outcomes and insights which this information provides. Only in this way will they be able to explain to others the source of problems, the origin of trends and the likely outcomes of past, current and future decisions. It is the written not verbal word which influences corporate decisions and the operations function's failure to use this medium contributes to its reactive stance.

The operations managers' view of themselves

Linked to the last point is the fact that operations managers view themselves as holding a reactive, corporate brief. They see their role as requiring them to react, as well as possible, to all that is asked of them and the production or service delivery system. Getting others out of difficulties is seen to be an integral and essential part of their task – and often one which they enjoy undertaking. On the other hand, rarely do they adequately contribute to or recognize their need to partake in strategic debate. Thus, they fail by default to provide appropriate inputs to corporate strategy formulation.

A company's view of the operations manager's role

Operations managers' view of their strategic role is reinforced by the company's view of their strategic contribution. Companies also see the operations role as short-term and reactive and, therefore, do not stress the long-term nature of this task.

Involved too late in the corporate debate

One understandable but inappropriate outcome of the way that operations managers' contributions are viewed is that these managers are not involved in corporate policy decisions until they have started to take shape. The result is that executives have less opportunity to contribute to decisions on strategic alternatives and, consequently, always appear to be complaining about the unrealistic demands made of them and the problems that invariably ensue.

For many businesses, corporate strategy comprises the independent inputs of different functions. However, this invariably leads to functional conflicts which, left unresolved, will result in inappropriate corporate decisions. Thus, given the large and fixed nature of operations investments, such procedures and outcomes will bind a company for years ahead. Linking these decisions to a company's markets is, therefore, then an essential step in strategy formulation.

Markets are inherently different and dynamic whilst operations management is inherently fixed

Overviewing a company's markets in terms of segments, regions, customers or generic products is necessary and appropriate in order to reflect essential marketing differences. However, if these descriptions go no further or are not presented to reflect other perspectives then they imply similarity (and hence a level of coherence) within each grouping for all functions besides marketing.

However, if you ask any executive 'Are all your businesses the same?' or 'Are all parts of any one business the same?' then the answer would be 'no' to both questions. Strategy outcomes need to reflect this. And, given the size and fixed nature of operations investments (that is, the inherent characteristics will not change unless a company deliberately changes them), it is totally appropriate to do this, indeed it is wholly essential. The large and fixed syndrome, whilst needing close regulation, receives inadequate attention. In today's markets, failing to link large investments to the markets they are designed to support is not only risky, it is also inexcusable.

Linking marketing and operations

The importance of linking operations and marketing is paramount. However, even though the logic for this is overpowering it typically does not take place. The main difficulty facing most companies is how to go about forging this link. Before addressing this, however, let us first consider a few examples that typify some of the dilemmas resulting from corporate failure to recognize the business dimensions of operations management, its inherent complexity and the fixed nature of its responses. The failure to appreciate that the level of differentiation required in operations is greater than in other functions has courted disaster in many companies, as the following examples testify.

Company A

Part of an international group, Company A faced a decline in markets and associated profits. To help address this it undertook a major internal review. The key changes concerned its two manufacturing plants. To provide a better orientation, it was decided to realign different products so that they would be made only at one or the other plant. The 'product orientation' resulted in each plant being allocated particular products and associated volumes. The overall result was that one plant had higher volumes spread over many fewer products. The second part of this strategic response to falling sales and profits was to invest in manufacturing both in terms of equipment and infrastructure. The programme comprised identical decisions which included investment in faster-throughput machines and the use of automatic links between processes designed to reduce indirect costs at various stages in the process. Whilst for one plant these decisions matched the needs and characteristics of its high-volume products and markets, for the other there was a significant mismatch. Two years on and £17 million later, whilst the first plant achieved higher than expected returns, the second was a long way from breaking even.

The process investments made in both plants were high-volume in nature – faster throughput speeds and linked processes leading to longer set-ups and the increased overall down-time which resulted. On the other hand, the loss-making plant's markets (determined by the product allocations) were characterized by low volumes necessitating many change-overs. Whilst the manufacturing strategy decisions were in line with the market characteristics in the one plant, they were out of line with the second.

Company B

As part of a drive to increase overall performance, a packing company undertook a major process investment. However, in order to meet corporate return on investment norms it was committed to increasing overall sales by some 40 per cent. However, achieving these much higher sales could only be made by entering price-sensitive markets with attendant high volumes and sales revenues. But its current markets were in the higher-quality segments and characterized by short lead times, fast customer response, low volume and high margins.

The consequences were significant. Not only did the company now have almost 30 per cent of its total orders with distinct low-cost needs but it also had to meet the delivery speed requirement of the remainder. For the new markets, manufacturing needed to provide low-cost support for which it required, amongst other characteristics, long production runs and stable schedules. For its existing markets it needed to continue to offer short lead-time responses to customers, with manufacturing providing support for this with an ability to change production schedules whilst accommodating the disruption that this introduced. The ramifications were substantial. Almost overnight the process investments and attendant market shift had introduced manufacturing conflict in a large part of its total business.

Company C

In a time of increasing competition, Company C decided to bring onto one site two separate businesses which, until then, had been sixty miles apart. Whilst one business was in high-value, low-volume, high-quality products, the business on the main manufacturing site was characterized by high-volume, price-sensitive items. Although some manufacturing processes were unique, most processes were similar in terms of technical provision. In addition to the obvious savings in overheads, part of the rationale for moving to one site was that the main unit had spare process capacity.

However, the company made two errors of judgement. First, it anticipated that whilst few skilled operators, supervisors and technical staff would move the sixty miles, the support requirements could be met by existing, main-site personnel. Second, it assumed that all process capacity was the same.

In the first instance, not only were the existing main-site skills inappropriate to both the product and process requirements of the new products, but the move introduced a conflicting set of quality conformance, volume and scheduling demands. In the second instance, the company soon became aware of the stark reality that high-volume process capacity is only of use for products with matching order-winning characteristics. Capacity availability does not have universal application.

Technical and business specifications

Leading on from the last example is the need for companies to identify that there exist both a technical and business specification.

The technical specification concerns just that. It identifies the technical parameters of a product/service embodied in an order or the technical specification of a process or item of equipment. However, the business specification embodies the non-technical dimensions so critical to the success of a business. These comprise issues around volume, the non-technical criteria which win orders (price, delivery reliability, delivery speed and quality) and which processes need to provide. It is these commercial/business-orientated dimensions which are not clearly identified and yet are fundamental to the overall success of a business. And, it is these which manufacturing provides with the engineering or technically-related dimensions supported by appropriate specialist functions.

Differentiating the task

The failure to adequately examine and explain markets typifies much of strategy debate. As a consequence, the level of detail essential to sound strategic formulation is not present. Instead, the outcomes are typified by characteristics such as the following.

Statements are general in nature

Most companies express their corporate strategy statements in general terms. This implies that the markets they serve are the same, and thus the essential differences which characterize these markets are not identified and so ignored. Typical forms comprise a mix of words and phrases which express similarity not difference. This also shows itself, as discussed in the next section, by a tendency to make all-embracing statements. But strategy debate should strive towards distilling the very essence of a company's various markets and thus help clarify, not disguise, strategic difference.

Descriptions have more than one meaning

The other characteristic of strategy debate is that the words used have more than one meaning. 'Critical success factors' and 'customer service' are two such phrases in general use. In embodying more than one meaning they become meaningless. The issue is not improving customer service but which dimension of customer service is to be improved. Unless debate goes down to this level then the essentials of strategy are lost.

Order-winners and qualifiers

The key to strategy debate is detail. To understand markets requires clear definition, which can only come from detailed discussions. But such detail is needed not at the operational but at the strategic level and requires clarity of outcomes. It is thus a distillation process with the end result representing the very essence of the business.

To achieve this, therefore, requires a move away from general statements in the following ways.

Words with only one meaning

Words must be clearly defined and contain only one meaning. They should then be used to reflect this one dimension thus giving essential clarity to the strategic debate which follows.

Order-winners and qualifiers

The second facet in achieving understanding is offered by separating relevant criteria into those which companies need to provide to get into and stay in markets (qualifiers) and those which, having qualified, will then win orders (order-winners).

Weighting order-winners and qualifiers

Further clarification comes from identifying the relative levels of importance differentiating one qualifier from another and one order-winner from another. This offers further clarification and thus helps further to distinguish criteria.

Criteria change over time

As markets are dynamic in nature, order-winners and qualifiers will change over time both in terms of the criteria themselves and the weightings they attract. To help identify these dynamics, markets are also reviewed in terms of the future and with the forward

projection reflecting the life cycles which characterize the particular
markets in question.

Achieving the link

A question posed earlier was, 'How do companies forge the link
between marketing and operations?' The answer is 'through the
business'. The underlying link between functions is the markets/
business in which a company competes. What should direct as well
as link functions is the need for all functions to support a company's
markets. This requires, therefore, that functions are party to
determining a company's markets and to reaching agreement as to
the qualifiers and order-winners appertaining to the various markets
to be served. This, in turn, is the basis on which functional
strategies need to be developed. It is a company's markets which all
functions need to support and it is this support which determines
the priorities, developments and investments within a function. In
this way businesses will be able to move away from functionally-
derived strategies to market-derived strategies. Only then will
functions be part of the essential corporate debate, be able to explain
the implications for and perspectives of each part of a business, be
party to the agreement on the markets in which the firm will
compete, help identify how the firm will compete in chosen markets
and develop strategies to provide appropriate levels and dimensions
of support.

   Figure 2.1 gives a framework for providing this essential debate
and, as the arrows indicate, the linkage is established through
determining and agreeing answers to the question 'How do pro-
ducts/services win orders in the marketplace?' On the one hand (and
represented by the arrow going from left to right), it represents the
position where operations managers are asking marketing questions
about a company's market(s). On the other hand (and represented
by the arrow going from right to left), the centre segment forms the
basis of the operations function's task in terms of what it needs to
provide as well as (qualifiers) and better than (order-winners)
relevant competitors.

How the framework operates

Strategy resolution is an iterative procedure, requiring debate and
further discussion over an extended period of time. A framework

such as that given in Figure 2.1 helps by providing a way of facilitating explanation. It does not imply that simply going sequentially through the following steps will lead to an outcome. As later figures show, it leads to debate between the major parts of a business, the mechanism for which is a discussion on and agreement about a company's markets.

The objective of using this framework is to produce an operations strategy for a business (steps 4 and 5). It will include a review of current and future products/services in terms of relevant qualifiers and order-winners both today and tomorrow. As investments in the operations function are both large and fixed, it is essential to look forward – the operations function has to support products/services over their entire life cycles. As product/service requirements change so will the operations managers' task, and the choice of process and infrastructure investments and developments needs to reflect this (steps 4 and 5). To reach steps 4 and 5 though, the first three steps will have to be taken.

With some understanding of what is to be achieved let us now work through each of the five steps whilst bearing in mind the iterative nature of this procedure when undertaking it in reality.

1 Corporate objectives	2 Marketing strategy	3 How do products/ services win orders in the marketplace?	Production/operations strategy	
			4 Process choice	5 Infrastructure
Growth Survival Profit Return on investment Other financial measures	Product/service markets and segments Range Mix Volumes Standardization versus customization Level of innovation Leader versus follower alternatives	Price Quality Delivery: Speed Reliability Demand increases Colour range Product/service range Design leadership Technical support supplied	Choice of various processes Trade-offs embodied in the process choice Process positioning Capacity: Size Timing Location Role of inventory in the process configuration	Function support Operations/planning and control systems Quality assurance and control Systems engineering Clerical procedures Payment systems Work structuring Organizational structure

Note: Although the steps to be followed are given as finite points in a stated procedure, in reality the process will involve statement and restatement, for several of these aspects will impinge on each other.

Source: Terry Hill, *Production/Operations Management: Text and cases* (2nd edn), Prentice Hall International, Hemel Hempstead, 1991, p. 26 (with permission).

Figure 2.1 Framework for reflecting production/operations strategy issues in corporate decisions

Step 1: Corporate objectives

Inputs into corporate strategy must be linked to the objectives of a business. Objectives are an essential part of forging strategic direction whilst providing targets against which actual performance can be measured. For each organization the objectives will be different. They will reflect the environment, markets, opportunities and preferences within the organization concerned.

Step 2: Marketing strategy

Linked closely to step 1 is the provision of a marketing strategy. This reviews current and future sales and so identifies anticipated areas of growth and decline and the current and future sales levels involved.

Step 3: How do products/services win orders in the marketplace?

In order to develop appropriate strategies (support for the agreed markets in terms of investments and developments) there needs to be a clear understanding and agreement on how the company competes in its various markets.

The outcome of this step, therefore, is to identify the different market segments in which a company competes and how orders are won in each of these. Often it is a case of which comes first, the chicken or the egg. This is because similarities and differences within and between segments are only revealed through debate. The procedure involved is lengthy. It starts best by asking marketing executives to segment the market as they perceive it. Having done this they are also asked to nominate products/services which represent each segment, and to determine the relevant order-winners and qualifiers for each segment with appropriate weightings.

The intention of this step is to provide a source of discussion which is supplemented by data analysis. The latter is a key part of this procedure and is based on the representative products/services already identified and reflects the relevant order-winners and qualifiers put forward. In this way views and opinions are checked by reality (for example, actual contribution/margin in terms of price; lead times in terms of delivery speed and actual performance in conformance quality and delivery reliability). The eventual outcome is similar to the examples shown in Tables 2.2 and 2.3. These illustrate how different order-winners and qualifiers relate to different products/services, the different weights which relate to relevant order-winners and how both the criteria and their weightings may change over time.

The outcome of this discussion, therefore, concerns identifying those criteria which are the task of the different functions to provide. This debate, therefore, is also a key feature in the development of the strategic response of other functions besides operations. But on reflection this would have to be so. Functions exist primarily to help fulfil the role of selling and providing customers with a company's products and services at an acceptable level of profit.

Step 4: Process choice

Operations can choose from a number of alternative processes to make the products or provide the services involved. The key to making this choice is the order quantities, the qualifiers and the order-winners involved. Each choice, however, has an inherent set

Table 2.2 The weekly volumes, order-winner weightings and qualifiers for three products considered representative of three product ranges

Order-winning criteria	Product, time-scale and weightings								
	Product A			Product B			Product C		
	1993	1994	1996	1993	1994	1996	1993	1994	1996
Design capability	–	–	–	40	–	–	–	–	–
Handling design modifications	–	–	–	–	20	–	20	–	–
Technical liaison support	–	–	–	20	20	–	20	–	–
UK-based supplier	10	–	–	10	10	10	20	–	–
Existing supplier	10	60	90	10	20	30	–	30	30
Price	60	40	10	20	30	60	30	40	40
Delivery – speed	20	–	–	–	–	–	10	30	30
– reliability	QQ	Q	–	–	QQ	QQ	QQ	QQ	QQ
Conformance quality	Q	Q	Q	–	QQ	Q	Q	Q	Q
Weekly volumes	2500	1500	50	–	300	700	3000	4000	4000

Note: Q denotes a qualifier and QQ, an order-losing sensitive qualifier.

Source: Terry Hill, *Manufacturing Strategy: The strategic management of the manufacturing function* (2nd edn), Macmillan, Basingstoke, 1993, p. 46 (with permission).

The Essence of Operations Management

Table 2.3   European Battery Company: order-winners and qualifiers for selected markets

	1991	1993	1995
Product Type A10			
Design	10	20	40
Conformance quality	20	20	–
Delivery – speed	70	40	30
– reliability	Q	QQ	QQ
Price	Q	20	30
Representative products A10, 60, 82 and 110			
Product Type B40			
Conformance quality	20	30	10
Delivery – speed	20	20	20
– reliability	QQ	QQ	QQ
Price	50	50	70
Technical field support	10	–	–
Representative products B40/6			
Product Type B500			
Design	50	50	50
Conformance quality	40	40	30
Delivery – speed	10	10	20
– reliability	QQ	QQ	QQ
Price	Q	Q	Q

Note: See Table 2.2.

Source: Hill, op. cit., 1993, p. 47 (with permission).

of trade-offs and thus companies need to reflect these (the business dimension) as well as the capability of a process to make the product/provide the service (the technical dimension) in their choice. In addition, it should be remembered that investments, once made, are unlikely to be repeated for some time (the fixed element of investments referred to earlier). Chapter 4 deals with these trade-offs in some detail.

Step 5: Operations infrastructure

Operations infrastructure comprises the non-process features, the soft side of the investments and developments within this function. As shown in Figure 2.1, it encompasses the procedures, systems, controls, payment schemes, work structuring alternatives, organizational issues and so on which make up the non-process aspects of operations.

However, as these are also large and fixed, the choosing in line with the needs of its markets is an essential part of the strategic response of the operations function.

The reality of strategic debate

As emphasized earlier, the framework and approach discussed in the last section do not imply that strategic debate is straightforward and follows a set of sequential steps. In reality, the debate is iterative in nature and comprises two major phases.

Phase 1

As shown in Figure 2.2, phase 1 of the review concerns assessing the operations function's current strategy in terms of existing and future markets. This allows for adjustments to be made in both process and infrastructure provision.

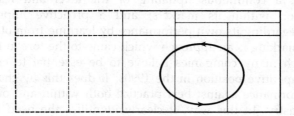

Source: Hill, op. cit., 1993, p. 52 (with permission).

Figure 2.2　Assessing the current strategic provision of operations in the light of the order-winners and qualifiers of current and future markets

Phase 2

As shown in Figure 2.3, phase 2 of the review concerns the mechanism for linking operations to the marketing function and corporate objectives. In this way, the implications for operations of current and proposed marketing strategies can be ascertained, as can the implications for marketing of current and proposed process and infrastructure developments and investments.

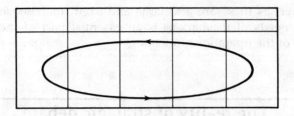

Source: Hill, op. cit., 1993, p. 55 (with permission).

Figure 2.3   Operations inputs into the corporate strategy debate

Benchmarking

The discussion on markets has so far emphasized an internal review and assessment in order to identify relevant order-winners and qualifiers. However, implied in this is the need for a company to assess and monitor its competitors. This is an essential part of strategy resolution as it provides two important dimensions for any company: a continuous updating of the level and features of competition within its markets; and a proactive improvement process regarding its own performance by learning from others.

Benchmarking is an approach which came to the fore in the 1980s and which many companies believe to be essential to enhancing their competitive position in the 1990s. It does this by checking its own performance against best practice both within and outside its own industry. In this way, it clearly identifies the need to assess market requirements, to differentiate importance and to establish the levels of performance necessary to remain or become competitive both today and in the future.

Benchmarking forces companies to look outwards and to recognize external perspectives as a key way to identify new targets. As benchmarking concerns the search for best practice, it involves continuously measuring a company's products, services and practices against competitors plus the leaders in any business sector. It is, however, not an end in itself but a means to help achieve superior levels of competitiveness.

This latter dimension enables a company to identify a broader range of potential best-in-class exemplars. This helps not only to improve the quality of its checking procedure but also to move from emulating the best to becoming an organization which changes the rules of the game by accomplishing pace-setting achievements.

Market competition is increasing on two dimensions – the nature of the order-winners and the level of performance within those criteria. As competition is a moving target, keeping pace and getting ahead need new ways of approaching this core strategic task. Keeping score and being ahead are becoming an essential part of that activity.

Market- or marketing-led?

Many companies do not keep in sharp focus the critical differences between being market-led and being marketing-led. To substitute the business (market) perspective with a function (marketing) perspective will invariably lead to distorted strategies and eventually to corporate disadvantage.

Unfortunately, in many businesses marketing is increasingly becoming characterized by the perceived role of creating ideas. Generating ideas often becomes an end in itself, with the rigour of testing business fit left to others. Many companies, however, fail to appreciate that the most significant orders are the ones to which a company says 'no'. For this marks the boundaries of the markets in which it competes and thus defines the context in which operations strategic response needs to be made.

The approach illustrated in Figure 2.1 facilitates these debates. Agreeing the relevant detail of markets creates appropriate strategic context. The procedure, therefore, helps orientate discussion towards corporate issues about the business itself and thus prepares the ground for essential corporate strategy resolution and agreement.

Key points review

To develop strategies which are meaningful and consistent requires the key functions to be party to that debate. Embracing these critical perspectives is the first step. From this comes agreement about the markets in which a company has selected to compete, what the key order-winners and qualifiers are within each segment and the functional strategies which need to be adopted.

The key features within this procedure are clarity of insights into markets, linking functional perspectives through the business debate and having sufficient calendar time to allow the debate and essential analyses to be completed.

Clarity

Clarity is the first step. Identifying order-winners and qualifiers, weighting their importance and assessing the way they change over time are essential steps. Moving away from generalities is a prerequisite in the procedure. Only then can insights into markets be clarified so as to allow differences to be identified.

Linking functional perspectives

Western organizations are controlled by using functions and specializations. One down side of this approach is that the parts of a business typically exist without sufficient cross-functional understanding. The outcome is that whereas linking core functions together is recognized as being essential, it is proving difficult to bring about. The key to achieving this is to relate issues through the medium of the business itself, as this is the essence of all activities and the common denominator for evaluating functional activities and developments. However, functions need to be party to agreeing the markets in which a company is to compete. Without this, the key functional perspectives will not be taken into account nor the implications for each function recognized and assessed. Functional strategies, however, not only form part of corporate strategy but also need to support the markets in an agreed and coherent fashion. When this has been accomplished then the elements of strategy will have been fulfilled.

Adequate calendar time

The procedure for strategic resolution concerns statement and restatement designed to arrive at decisions which best suit the business as a whole. In this way, therefore, companies are able to move away from functionally-based strategy-making, recognizing the fact that operations strategy is not the operations function's but the business's operations strategy. The same argument applies to marketing strategy and the strategies of other functions. Only through debate and agreement can adequate levels of understanding be achieved. The earlier key points of clarity and functional linking are part of achieving this. The third is providing adequate calendar time for the issues to be raised, clarity to be established, implications to be assessed and agreement to be reached on what will be best for the business as a whole. Companies have to appreciate that the time needed to arrive at fully understood and appropriate strategies cannot be short-circuited. A one-off strategy weekend will only result in superficial insights and hence inadequate outcomes.

3

Operations and design

For decades, engineers have been exhorted to design for operations. The plea has been commonplace and the rationale behind it needs little explanation. The impact of product/service design on material costs, staffing levels and the ease of provision in terms of process flexibility is considerable. To these significant business perspectives has been added the dimension of product/service development lead times which, by the early 1990s, was emerging as an important order-winner in many markets. The significance of linking design to operations has now, therefore, taken on a further competitive dimension, thus reinforcing this already critical relationship.

Operations and design

As outlined above, the links between operations and design are fundamental to the overall success of many businesses. The need to link these two important functions is, therefore, not for the benefit of operations but for the benefit of business itself. Thus, the plea to design for operations is, in fact, a plea to design for the business.

As stressed in the last chapter, the links between and common goals of functions are forged through supporting agreed markets. As the following sections show, the many design-related order-winners and qualifiers are either supported directly by design or directly impact the operations function. Awareness of providing support for strategic market needs must then be at the forefront of priorities and decisions.

Design leadership

It is not unusual for companies to be in markets the relevant order-winners for which are not directly related to operations. In these types of markets, operations will typically be required to support one or more qualifiers.[1]

One order-winner which may often create such a situation is that of design leadership. This concerns one of the design function's principal roles – that of developing products/services in terms of features, aesthetics, perceived levels of design in specification, and reliability (including costs) whilst in service.[2]

The importance of product/service design is universally recognized. Markets can be dominated by this dimension and creating unique designs, particularly in the past, has been considered the principal order-winning provision to be made by this function. Couple this with a company's desire to establish a brand name for its products/services (where design's role is supplemented by factors such as advertising and the growth/maintenance of market share) and orders will, at least in part, be won due to this dimension.

Product/service development lead times

Reducing lead times in the manufacturing process or service delivery system has already been highlighted as an increasingly important order-winner (pp. 20–1). Similarly, speed to market with new product/service designs and developments is becoming a significant competitive factor in today's markets. The increasing priority of speed is based on the recognition that it can simply negate the competition. Examples of improvement are given in Table 3.1, and the results speak for themselves.

Table 3.1 Superfast innovators

Company	Product	Development time (years)	
		old	new
Honda	Cars	5.0	3.0
AT & T	Telephones	2.0	1.0
Navistar	Trucks	5.0	2.5
Hewlett-Packard	Computer printers	4.5	1.8

Source: B. Dumaine, 'How managers can succeed through speed', *Fortune* (13 February 1989), pp. 54–9 (with permission).

These reductions come principally from the following three sources. As would be expected, aspects within each are, however, linked one with another and thus getting the most benefit will be achieved through working both on each facet and on the areas of overlap.

Reducing the length of each step

The steps involved in designing a new product/service are systematically reviewed in order to find ways to complete the work in less time. This includes a systematic review of work methods and the setting of target times for completing the tasks involved.

Simultaneous engineering

In many companies, stages in product/service developments have been traditionally scheduled to be undertaken on a sequential basis (that is, step 2 starts when step 1 is completed and so on). However, by reviewing each set of tasks, companies find that one step can in fact be started before the 'previous' step is completed. The reduction of overall lead time can be dramatic, as shown in the example given in Figure 3.1. The principle which leads companies to change, where possible, from a sequential to a parallel format in completing some or all steps in the development process is known as *simultaneous* or *concurrent engineering*.[3]

Changing roles, perceptions and expectations

The final aspect concerns changing the roles, perceptions and expectations of those involved in completing the tasks and their relationships with each other. One example which illustrates this is the role of design engineers.

The expectation of Western designers is to develop a product/service which requires little or no modification. As perfection is rarely, if ever, achieved, any changes to be made are typically identified in the later phases of the total development procedure. Also part of the typical design function's attitude in these circumstances is an inbuilt resistance to changes suggested by others. The result is a long, initial design phase subsequently further increased by an inherent resistance to embrace suggested changes as they arise.

The Japanese alternative is based on a different set of expectations. Knowing that to design perfection is impossible, they do not attempt to achieve this. The result is that designers conclude their

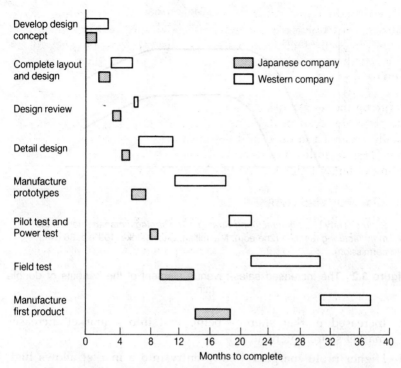

Source: G. Stalk, Jr and T. M. Hout, *Competing against Time: How time-based competition is reshaping global markets*, Free Press, New York, 1990, p. 188, Exhibit 4-1 *(with permission)*

Figure 3.1 Improving response time in new product development – mechanical transmissions

proposals much more quickly than their Western counterparts and, being more ready to accept change, respond to suggestions more willingly. The result is a significant, overall reduction in development lead times.

Companies which achieve these lead-time reductions enjoy a number of distinct advantages including the benefits of double gain. Being first in the market brings advantages of both higher volumes and higher margins (the benefits of double gain) as follows:

- Product/service life cycles are extended – being first in the market does not reduce the life cycle of a product/service. The result is that more sales are made where a company is first in the market (see Figure 3.2).

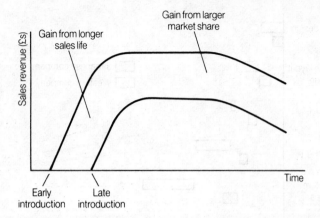

Source: Terry Hill, *Manufacturing Strategy: The strategic management of the manufacturing function* (2nd edn), Macmillan, Basingstoke, 1993, p. 88 (with permission).

Figure 3.2   The increased sales-revenue element of the benefits of double gain

- Increased market share – being first into a market increases market share potential.

- Higher profit margins – early entry into a market allows high prices in the early stages (see Figure 3.3) and cost-reduction opportunities later on as the market develops and grows. Evidence clearly shows that as experience accumulates, performance improves, and the experience curve is the quantification of this improvement. The basic phenomenon of the experience curve is that the cost of making a product or providing a service falls in a regular and predictable way as the total quantity processed increases. The characteristic decline in cost or price per unit is between 20 and 30 per cent for each doubling of cumulative quantities produced or provided.[4]

Price

Design not only concerns functionality but also has a critical impact on product/service costs. With direct materials typically accounting for 35–50 per cent of the total,[5] opportunities to reduce costs at source are substantial. In addition, the issue of low cost requirements also reinforces the role of design in reducing staff costs through increased automation and other labour-saving opportunities.

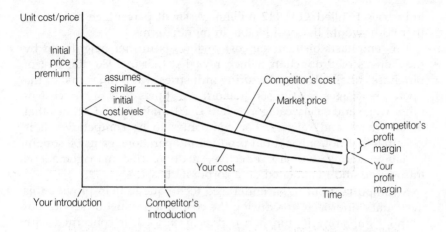

Source: Hill, op. cit., 1993, p. 89 (with permission).

Figure 3.3 The higher profit-margin element of the benefits of double gain

These critical, cost-related links can be achieved in a number of ways. With the need agreed, companies must pursue some or all of the following approaches in order to secure cost-reduction opportunities as part of a continuous improvement approach.[6]

Standardization
The concept of standardization concerns using the same materials, components, subassemblies and/or modules within the design of two or more products/services.

Standardized components and subassemblies can be used to make finished items that are different in appearance, performance and specification. This approach can be formalized into providing modular designs such that a variety of final products/services use only a few basic components. The result is lower costs without detracting from the overall performance of the product or service.

Value engineering and value analysis
Whilst the price of materials, components and services is the concern of purchasing, another important factor determining an organization's material costs is how well it utilizes these materials. In 1986 the cost of purchases made by all UK manufacturing

industries totalled £132,112 million. A small percentage reduction, therefore, would be considerable in money terms.

This emphasis on material cost reviews is further heightened by the Census of Production, which revealed that in 1986, the cost of purchases of all UK manufacturing industries was 5 times that of the operators' wages (at £26,566 million), 7.7 times that of the cost of other wage and salary categories (at £17,201 million) and 3 times that of all wages and salaries. For companies to be competitive, it is essential that not only should production/operations gains be sought in labour terms, but also effective, material cost management is introduced and maintained on a corporate basis.

An important but often underused technique to help provide this systematic approach to reducing the cost of a product or service but without impairing its function is *value analysis*. It is concerned with the methodical examination of each component, product or service without reducing its functional value.[7] The term 'value engineering' is often used synonymously with value analysis but, strictly speaking, the former refers to the use of this technique in the initial stages of product/service design.

Value analysis considers the functions which the components, products or services are intended to perform. It then reviews the present design in order to provide these functions at a lower material and labour cost, without reducing the value. As Lawrence Miles (who developed these concepts) said:

> On average, one fourth of [operations] cost is unnecessary. The additional cost continues because of the patterns and habits of thought, because of personal limitations, because of difficulties in promptly disseminating ideas and because today's thinking is based on yesterday's knowledge.[8]

The causes of unnecessary costs which may result from the design function include the following:

* adopting a safety-first policy which results in overspecification;
* preoccupation with meeting the functional specification and, consequently, an undue concern for value-for-money issues;
* failure to specify clearly (especially in services) what constitutes a product/service;
* lack of current information being available to designers;
* functional specialisms which help create barriers between design, purchasing, operations and sales.

Quality conformance[9]

Although the task of quality conformance (that is, making a product or providing a service to an agreed specification) is the principal task of operations, the design of the product/service will have a direct bearing on how easy/difficult that is to achieve consistently. Over-compensating (as discussed in the last section) by designers may also lead to creating requirements which are unnecessarily exacting and which place higher demands on operations with provision to specification consequences.

Product/service range

The increasing level of product/service diversification is an important factor in today's increasingly competitive markets. Central to this provision is the design function, the pressure on which will vary from market to market, and the execution of which is central to a company's ability to remain competitive. The tendency for Western designers to be more interested in functionality than in the commercial facets of design is in marked contrast to competitors, particularly the Japanese. As Hiroyuki Yoshida, head of Toyota's design centre, reflected:

> Whatever the merits of a design, it has to be robust enough to go through our engineering and manufacturing system. The commercial point of design has not been lost. We are in the business to make low cost, high quality cars for a mass market. We are making cars, not art.[10]

Operations management's responses to supporting product/service range

Earlier the benefits of variety were emphasized. Thus, whereas the last section describes essential approaches in order to test the benefits of supporting a given product/service range, it is equally essential for companies to work hard at coping effectively with a wide variety of items.

Design-related responses

Part of the response to coping effectively with variety needs to be addressed at the design stage. The use of standardization and modular designs helps minimize the disadvantages of wide-range approaches. It enables a level of diversification to be met without the attendant drawbacks of low volumes and associated costs.

Operations-related responses

Being able to support a wide range of products/services can bring with it a distinct market advantage. Furthermore, the markets of the 1990s will continue to be characterized by difference and not similarity. Hence, it is important for operations to be able to create conditions which minimize the effects of this provision.

One important development in this regard is the continuous reduction in set-up or make-ready times. By systematically reducing the length of time it takes to complete the pre-processing tasks, the operations function is able to cope with the correspondingly lower volumes which, typically, go hand-in-hand with these developments.

Variety reduction

With the provision of a wide product/service range goes the assumption of market benefits. It is important, therefore, continuously to appraise the width of range offered. One approach is known as *variety reduction*.

In a company's current range, some items will generate higher sales and/or higher profits than others. Moreover, the costs incurred and efforts involved in providing and selling the lower contributors are disproportionately higher than for other products/services. Consequently, looking closely at the contribution that these items make should form part of a continuous review in order to move towards a reduction in uneconomic variety.

The approach within variety reduction is to list all products/ services in descending order of sales value. This often reveals that about 20 per cent of items account for about 80 per cent of sales revenue. This is known as the 80/20 rule, and illustrates the Pareto principle. The next step is to review the least-value items over the last three or four years to see if the trend is upward, level or downward. Further checks are then made on the level and downward items to see if their contribution can be improved by increasing price, reducing costs or some combination of both. If this action does not bring about the required changes, then phasing out such items should be considered.[11]

Examples of uneconomic variety are by no means confined to the more sophisticated end of the product/service continuum. Here current ranges are often subjected to the phenomenon of creeping variety as variations are provided to meet the particular needs of customers' diverse range of requirements. In a recent study,

> Unilever was surprised to discover that it was using 85 varieties of flavouring in the chicken soups it sells in Europe and making Cornetto ice creams (supposedly a standardised Euro-product) in 15 different cone shapes . . . changing tastes and fiercer competition have compelled (the company) to ask whether it needs (or can afford) such variety . . . the company has concluded that its product range has evolved less in response to the vagaries of consumer taste than because each of its traditionally autonomous national subsidiaries had been left to do things in its own way.[12]

Eliminating inefficient duplication has been one way in which Unilever has turned to reshape its food business as part of an effort to improve overall performance and remain competitive.

Key points review

As emphasized earlier, Western corporate appeals to design for operations have been more in the category of exhortation than accomplishment. However, in the 1990s, pressure on design-related order-winners and qualifiers will, in many market segments, continue to be an important competitive factor. Thus, design's role in the total corporate response to increasingly competitive markets is fundamental in more ways than one.

Criteria such as design leadership, product/service development lead times, conformance quality and price are at the very core of the competitive features of many markets. And the role of design and its links with operations are at the centre of this provision. Companies, however, need to move rapidly towards the realization of these opportunities. Faced in many markets with increasing competitive threats and pressures, it is no longer the case that these developments offer a distinct advantage but more a matter of first having to catch up with the competition. For many companies criteria which were once in the category of order-winners are now prerequisites.

They need to recognize, therefore, that even to be considered there are many dimensions on which they must first qualify.

Notes

1. This is more fully examined in Chapter 3 of Terry Hill, *Manufacturing Strategy: The strategic management of the manufacturing function* (2nd edn), Macmillan, Basingstoke, 1993.
2. Refer to D. A. Garvin 'Competing on the Eight Dimensions of Quality', *Harvard Business Review* (November/December 1987), pp. 101–9.
3. For further details on simultaneous engineering, see Chapter 11, 'Managing Product and Process Development Projects', in J. D. Blackburn (ed.) *Time-based Competition: The next background in American manufacturing*, Irwin, Homewood, Ill., 1991, pp. 304–39, and J. Mortimer and J. Hartley, 'Managing in the 90s: Simultaneous engineering', Department of Trade and Industry Publication, June 1991.
4. The concept of experience curves is dealt with in more detail in Terry Hill, *Manufacturing Strategy: Text and cases*, Irwin, Homewood, Ill., 1989, pp. 113–35.
5. See Garvin, op. cit.
6. See Terry Hill, *Production/Operations Management: Text and cases* (2nd edn), Prentice Hall International, Hemel Hempstead, 1991, pp. 91–3 and 353–6.
7. Value analysis is defined in BS 3138 (1979) 'Glossary of Terms used in Word Study and Organisation and Methods 33006' as: 'a systematic interdisciplinary examination of factors affecting the cost of a product or service, in order to devise means of achieving the specified purpose most economically at the required standard of quality and reliability'.
8. L. D. Miles, *Techniques of Value Analysis and Engineering*, McGraw-Hill, Maidenhead, 1961.
9. See Garvin, op. cit.
10. Quoted in C. Leadbeater, 'Toyota's Conundrum: creating a global car for a niche market', *Financial Times* (17 July 1991), p. 16.
11. For further details see Hill, op. cit., 1991, pp. 43–4.
12. G. de Jonquieres, 'Just One Cornetto . . .', *Financial Times* (28 October 1991), p. 14.

4

The delivery system

Chapter 2 stressed the need for companies to place their investments and developments in the operations function within an appropriate strategic context. These investments concern the choice of process by which products would be made and services delivered and also the operations infrastructure which comprises supporting systems, procedures and functions to help manage, control and improve the management of the operations task.

This chapter addresses the process or hardware decisions within a business. It reviews the important trade-offs which need to be understood and made by businesses in line with the sets of order-winners and qualifiers which relate to their markets. In addition, it introduces issues concerning capacity in terms of its use, provision and timing.

The transformation process

The operations function is responsible for producing the goods or providing the services that the company sells in the marketplace. Common to all the diverse range of goods and service activities is the conversion process illustrated in Figure 4.1. The operations task concerns managing the transformation process which takes inputs and converts them into outputs, together with the various support functions associated with completing this basic task. The level of complexity within operations depends on factors such as the

• size of the organization;

39

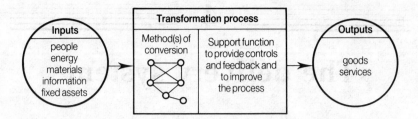

Source: Terry Hill, *Production/Operations Management: Text and cases* (2nd edn), Prentice Hall International, Hemel Hempstead, 1991, p. 57 (with permission).

Figure 4.1　The operations function

- complexity of the products/services involved;
- make or buy decision influencing the made/provided in-house content of the task.

The operations process concerns transforming inputs into outputs and is accomplished by a combination of labour and processes/ equipment within the delivery system. The remainder of the chapter addresses the issues of choosing processes and developing capacity in line with the market needs of a company.

Process choice

One of the key perspectives of the operations function is the need to recognize that it is not a technical or engineering-related function but a business-related function. In any company you will invariably find that the operations function is separated from the relevant engineering or technical services within the organization. This separation is both appropriate and correct, for whereas the operations function's task is to make products and/or provide services (business-related activities) the role of engineering/technical functions is to provide specialist advice in terms of investments, developments and support activities (technically-related activities).

　In the important decisions concerning processes, therefore, whereas the technical role is to ensure that the process is able to meet the product/service specification, meeting the specification (conformance quality) and providing any other relevant order-winners and qualifiers are the tasks of the operations function. In this way both the technical and business dimensions of products and services are provided within a company, with the relevant functions involved having a different orientation, mandate and strategic task.

The need for a business to understand fully the characteristics of the operations function's investments in terms of both their technical and business dimensions is simply due to the fact they embody two distinct characteristics. All the investments will be both large and fixed. Large in terms of the size of the financial investment and fixed in that it will typically take companies a long time to get into and a long time to change the investments involved.

Process alternatives

The transformation process and methods of conversion to produce goods or provide services will actually be an interrelated set of processes feeding into one another as part of the total task. There are five different ways of making products or providing services, together with a number of hybrids which result from mixing together aspects of two of these classic systems. Typically firms will have a mix of two or more of these processes in order to meet the varying needs of the products/services they provide and sell.

Project

Organizations that sell large-scale, complex products or services which cannot be physically moved once completed will normally provide these on a project basis. Product examples include civil engineering contracts and aerospace programmes. Service examples include management consultancy assignments involving corporate policy issues and organizational development, and a large banquet supplied to the customer's own premises. This process is concerned with the provision of a unique product or service which requires large-scale inputs to be coordinated to achieve the customer's requirement. The resource inputs will normally be taken to the point where the product is to be built or service provided.

All the activities, including support functions, will normally be controlled as a total system for the duration of the project and under the direction of a coordinating team. Similarly, resources will be allocated for the duration of the project and these, like the supporting functions, will be reallocated once their part of the task is complete or at the end of the project.

The operations manager's problem, then, is one of coordinating a large number of interrelated activities and resources in such a way as to achieve the customer's requirements whilst minimizing costs through the process.

Jobbing, unit or one-off

A jobbing process is chosen to meet the one-off or small-order requirements of customers. The product or service involved is of an individual nature, and small enough to be moved from where it was made/provided to where the customer needs it. Product examples include purpose-built equipment, hand-made, built-in furniture and hand-made shoes. Services examples include tailor-made management development programmes and the design and installation of computer systems.

Although some of these products and services may be made or provided on site, usually they are completed in-house and then transported to a given location.

Jobbing requires the supplier to interpret the design and specification of the task, applying high-level skills in the conversion. Normally, one or a small group of skilled people will be responsible for completing all or most of the product/service.

Jobbing versus job shop

It seems pertinent here to draw the distinction between jobbing and a job shop. The former has already been described as one way of making a product or providing a service. It is, therefore, an operations process description. A job shop, on the other hand, is a commercial description of a business and usually implies customized products/services often of a low-volume, non-repeat nature. A classic example is a jobbing printer, which refers to a company engaged in printing customized products which are often low-volume and may not be required again. However, the process used in such a business would not be jobbing but invariably would be batch, as explained below.

Specials, customized products/services and standard products/ services

Similarly, it is important at this time to distinguish between specials, customized products/services and standard products/services. The word 'special' is used to describe the 'one-off' provision referred to earlier in this section (the product/service will not again be required in its exact form, or if it is the demand will tend to be irregular, with long time periods between one order and the next). The phrase 'standard product/service' means the opposite – the demand for the product/service is repeated and thus warrants investment.

The word 'customized' refers to a product/service which is made to a customer's specification. However, the demand for such products/services can be either special (not repeated) or standard (repeated) in nature. An example of the latter is the many forms of packaging which by their very nature are customized (for example, the customer's name and details are printed on a label or carton) and characterized by demand which is high and invariably of a repeat nature – operations factors which will be reflected in the chosen process and would invariably be batch.

The key difference to operations concerns the repeat nature of a product/service. Only with high-volume (often repeat) products/ services will investment in all its forms be appropriate in terms of both process and infrastructure.

Batch

In a batch process, similar items required in larger volumes than in jobbing will be provided. First, the product/service task is characteristically divided into appropriate stages. Then, each order is processed by setting up the first step of the process to complete the first stage of the task. Each item in an order is then completed at this stage and then the next step of the process is set up and the second stage of the task is completed, and so on. Thus, capacity at each stage in the process is used and reused to meet the different requirement of different orders.

Examples in manufacturing include printing (as explained in the last section) and moulding. In both instances a machine will be set up with the appropriate cylinder or lithographic mat or the relevant mould to make the desired product and the required amount is then produced. In each instance, when the required quantity has been made the printing or moulding machine will be stopped and reset for the next job. The essential characteristic of batch, therefore, is that to produce another product or provide another service, the process has to be stopped and reset. Product examples include printed labels, car components, domestic products for the kitchen or bathroom and items for the office. Other typical batch manufacturing processes are making metal products, casting and other forming processes. Service examples include a computer bureau that processes the work of several clients on the same hardware, and large clerical tasks. In each instance, the job is broken down into its constituent operations and one order quantity of work is completed by one person and so on.

Line

With further increases in volume, investment is made to provide a process that is dedicated to the needs of a single or small range of products and, very occasionally, services. This repetitive process is one, therefore, in which the product(s) or service(s) are processed with each product/service passing through the same sequence of operations. The essential characteristic of line (compared to batch), therefore, is that to produce another product or provide another service, the process does not have to be stopped and reset. Product examples include domestic appliances and motor vehicles. Services are not widespread but include certain preparatory operations in fast-food restaurants such as McDonald's. A further example is provided by Dr Svyatoslav Fyoderov's Institute of Eye Microsurgery in Moscow which uses the process for the treatment of myopia. Using laser technology and assembly line methods, surgeons at the Institute cure myopia using the classic principles of a line process.

Continuous processing

With continuous processing, one or several basic materials are processed through successive stages and refined into one or more products, for example, petrochemicals. Because the costs of starting up the process are inhibiting, the process will have been designed to run all day and every day with minimum shut-downs. The materials are transferred automatically from one part of the process to the next with the labour tasks being predominantly concerned with system monitoring. This type of process is not used in the provision of a service.

The reality of process choice

So far it has been implied that companies are able to select from the whole range of processes and available hybrids. However, in reality this is not so. Both technical and business constraints exist which limit suitable alternatives, as explained below.

Project and continuous processing

When considering the choice of these processes the nature of the product or service will also be an overriding factor. This is because the 'difficult to move' characteristic of project and the 'fluid-type' characteristic of continuous processing will limit the suitability and feasibility of these choices, respectively. And so, companies prefer not to use the project process if it can be avoided due to the ineffectiveness which comes from having to set up and then dismantle facilities at the start and end of a job. Hence, more and more subassemblies, sections of buildings or large parts and structures are made elsewhere (and using processes other than project) and then transported to the site where they will be installed or form part of a large permanent structure. Likewise, for continuous processing to be a feasible choice the product would have to be such as to move easily through tubes or pipes.

Jobbing, batch and line

As most products/services are movable once completed and many products cannot be moved through tubes, most companies choose from jobbing, batch and line processes.

However, a review of these latter alternatives reveals further limitations on what would be appropriate for most businesses. Today, few companies have products which attract volumes which justify the dedicated characteristics of line. Similarly, few organizations serve markets in which products/services are truly special, will not be provided again and thereby would be best served by a jobbing process. Thus, for most companies batch processes are the only appropriate alternative. As illustrated by the elongated representation of batch (see Figure 4.2), companies use these processes to accommodate the requirements of a wide range of volumes. But companies need to recognize that low-, medium- and high-volume batch processes handle a very wide range of volumes with correspondingly different order-winners. For companies, therefore, to assume that the choice of one process, even with a single category such as batch, will provide support for the level of diversity associated with a normal range of products/services, is a mistake. The arguments of the early proponents of flexibility have given way

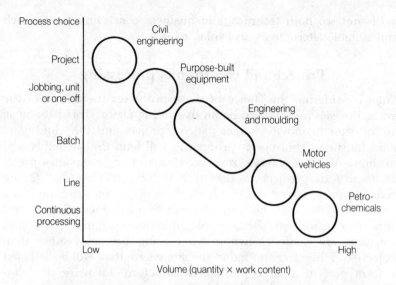

Volume (quantity × work content)

Source: Terry Hill, *Manufacturing Strategy: The strategic management of the manufacturing function* (2nd edn), Macmillan, Basingstoke, 1993, p. 114 (with permission).

Figure 4.2 Choice of process reflecting the link with volumes

to the outcomes of reality. For example, flexible manufacturing systems, sold as a panacea for handling the increasing variety of markets, have proven to be inappropriate. Why? Simply, there is no process which can cope with a very wide range of volumes and associated order-winners and be as efficient and effective as a process which is designed to meet the requirements of a much more limited volume range. Matching market dimensions and process characteristics is an essential business requirement. The difficulties in doing this are the realities of manufacturing investments – they are both large and fixed and so companies do not typically reinvest a second time. Thus, it is essential that companies know what they are buying in terms of the needs of their current and future markets.

The fixed nature of process investments

Within any business, the inherent characteristics of its markets are directly opposite to the inherent characteristics of its operations function. Whilst the former are inherently dynamic, the latter are inherently fixed – no more so than with regard to process investments.

The impact of these phenomena is further heightened by the way in which organizations typically approach these decisions. In order to minimize the total investment to be committed to the support of a product or service, companies tend to invest only once. Their choice reflects the anticipated sales of a product or service over a given period. The use of forecast volumes on which to base these key decisions is reflected in the format provided by Figure 4.2, which illustrates the volume relationship with the choice of process.

However, when undertaking these decisions companies often fail to take into account the fixed nature of the process investment it will be making – fixed in that it will not change unless companies reinvest in developing the process in a given way. For many, the reason for this is their failure to recognize and, therefore, discuss and assimilate the business trade-offs involved in the alternatives from which they can choose. The outcome is that the essential link between current and future market needs and the mix of trade-offs embodied in the process choice(s) made are typically not reconciled. How these can be recognized ahead of time and thus influence the investment decision itself or can be recognized as having taken place over time and thus stimulate reinvestment in order to change the characteristics involved is based on an essential understanding of the nature and choices which are involved.

Trade-offs of process choice

Companies invest in processes to meet the needs of their products or services. As already explained, the choice they can make is constrained by the engineering dimension (the process will have to be able to meet the product/service specification) and those dimensions detailed under the section 'The reality of process choice' (pp. 44–6).

Outside these constraints companies then need to decide which process best suits their needs. It is at this juncture that the engineering dimension finishes and the manufacturing/business dimension starts. Phase 1 in process selection is to assess the volumes involved and the process choices available. Phase 2 is to check the trade-offs which would result from the alternatives on hand and assess which mix would best meet the market needs of the business. Figure 4.3 illustrates how a company will first decide on the process using the volume dimension (points A1 and B1) but then needs to recognize that its choice will automatically result in the provision of different sets of trade-offs shown here as A2 and B2.

These trade-offs present a way for a company to assess which process decisions best fit its current and future markets. However, as companies will typically compete in markets which are different, the analyses described here will need to be undertaken for each market served by a company. The completed analyses review market characteristics and differences while also assessing the implications for relevant parts of the business including changes in capacity, planning and control systems, inventory levels and key elements of infrastructure. Assessing the implications for the overall business then becomes the relevant output of this strategic review.

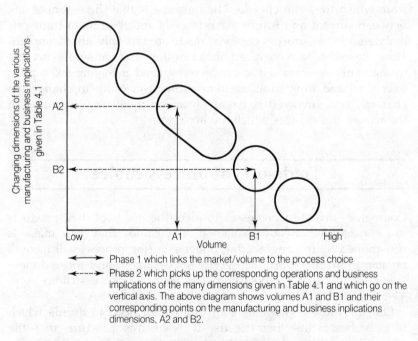

←——→ Phase 1 which links the market/volume to the process choice

←---→ Phase 2 which picks up the corresponding operations and business implications of the many dimensions given in Table 4.1 and which go on the vertical axis. The above diagram shows volumes A1 and B1 and their corresponding points on the manufacturing and business inplications dimensions, A2 and B2.

Source: Hill, op. cit., 1993, p. 117 (with permission).

Figure 4.3   Process choice – linking the engineering dimension to the manufacturing/business dimension

The sections which follow explain these trade-offs in some detail based upon the selected dimensions in Table 4.1, which reflect important characteristics of a business.[1]

Products/services and markets

Project/jobbing processes tend, by definition, to be chosen to provide specials competing predominantly on aspects such as unique skills offering and delivery speed rather than price. As a provider of non-standard products/services the organization will offer a diverse range of products/services in order to meet widely different customer requirements. For this reason a company sells a set of capabilities rather than a standard product/service.

In line and continuous processing, the opposite end of the spectrum prevails. Products and services are highly standardized and tend to compete primarily on price. Little, if any, accommodation will be provided in the process to meet product/service change and even where there is (as with motor vehicles) it tends to be designed to meet the more superficial aspects of product/service change such as colour and trim, with extras being provided only within a supplier's own list of options. A customer requiring an option other than from the supplier's approved list will need to arrange a retro-fit.

Batch processes occupy the middle position. With increases in volume, an organization will start to move from low-volume to high-volume markets. When this happens, price increasingly becomes an order-winner in relevant segments, with corresponding movement on the other dimensions given in Table 4.1.

Operations

In project and jobbing the product/service provided is one-off (unique). Thus, the operations task will be variable, often not fully known, and the process will need to be flexible using universal/general-purpose equipment and skilled labour.

With line and continuous processing these perspectives change. This choice is made to support high-volume, standard products/services usually competing on price. The task of the operations

Table 4.1 Selected business implications of process choice[2]

Business dimensions		Project	Jobbing	Batch	Line	Continuous processing
PRODUCTS/SERVICES AND MARKETS						
Product/service	type	Special	Special	→	Standard	Standard
	range	High diversity	Wide	→	Narrow	Narrow
Customer order size		Small	Small	→	Large	Very large
Level of product/service change required in the process		High	High	→	Low	Nil
Level of product/service introductions		High	High	→	Low	Very low
What does a company sell?		Capability	Capability	→	Standard products/services	Standard products/services
How does an organization win orders?	typical order-winners	Unique skills, delivery speed	Unique skills, delivery speed	→	Price	Price
	typical qualifiers	Delivery reliability, quality and price	Delivery reliability, quality and price	Delivery reliability and quality	Delivery reliability and quality	Delivery reliability and quality

OPERATIONS				
Process technology	Universal	General-purpose	Dedicated	Dedicated
Flexibility	Flexible	Flexible	Inflexible	Inflexible
Volumes	Low	Low	High	Very high
Changes in capacity	Incremental	Incremental	Stepped	New facility
Key operations task	Meet delivery schedule	Meet delivery schedule	Cost reduction	Cost reduction
ORGANIZATIONAL IMPLICATIONS				
Coordination — customers	Low degree	Low degree	Highly organized	Highly organized often with forward integration
Coordination — suppliers	Variable	Low degree	Highly organized	Highly organized
Organizational — control	Decentralized	Decentralized	Centralized	Centralized
Organizational — style	Informal	Informal	Bureaucratic	Bureaucratic
Dominant operations management perspective	Technology	Technology	Business/people	Technology

Source: adapted from Hill, op. cit., 1991, Tables 4.1–4.4, pp. 61–9.

function will, therefore, be well defined, using dedicated plant and equipment, with changes in capacity being of a stepped nature.

Batch processes are again the transition between low- and high-volume activities. They may, therefore, tend towards either jobbing or line and contain a mix of the characteristics involved.

Organizational implications

In project and jobbing processes the nature of the task tends to be for unique, variable operations providing flexible responses. The organization more suited to these requirements is one of decentralized control with a more entrepreneurial style. Opportunities to forge a high degree of supplier and customer coordination will normally be limited. However, operations managers would be expected to advise in areas of process technology and their professional background would, therefore, be in an appropriate technology.

With line and continuous processing, these characteristics will tend to be reversed. The highly standardized, cost-dominated tasks will be more suited to centralized control and a bureaucratic style. The dominant operations management perspective will change between line and continuous processing. The management skills as companies move to line processing will become much more business- and people-orientated because of the high volumes and large investments, control requirements and numbers of staff involved. Thus, the investment that has gone into the process will have decreased the technical but increased the business and managerial tasks involved in managing the operations task. With continuous processing the trends as described for line processing will reverse. The process will be technology-based and the tasks controlled by people with a knowledge of the technology and, as with line, supported by a high level of supporting staff.

Again, the transition comes in batch. The lower the volume requirement within the batch process, the more akin the infrastructure requirements will be to those of jobbing. The higher the volume, the more akin the requirements will be to line.

Hybrid processes

As mentioned earlier, many companies have developed hybrid processes, the reason for which is to provide a process which better reflects their needs in terms of being able to support the characteristics of their markets. Some comprise a mix of two of the five classic processes, others are developments within an existing process type, often based on the use of numerical control (NC) machines.[2] Some of the more important hybrid developments are now explained, and to help position these in relation to the classic processes they are included together in Figure 4.4. However, the list includes some (for example, machining centres) which have received general application and are provided as standard items[3] from a supplier's catalogue. Finally, there are few, if any, examples of services using these processes. Throughout, therefore, the discussion will centre around the making of products.

Finally, as with all hybrids there is a 'root stock'. Thus, although each hybrid format will comprise a mix of two process types, it will still be classified as belonging to one or the other. This phenomenon is highlighted by the section headings 'batch-related' and 'line-

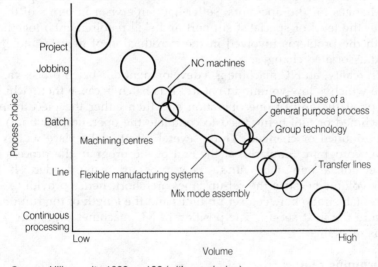

Source: Hill, op. cit., 1993, p. 132 (with permission).

Figure 4.4 The positions of some hybrid processes in relation to the five classic choices of process

related' which follow. Within these sections the hybrids described have batch and line 'roots', respectively. What happens is that each hybrid alters some of the trade-offs described in Table 4.1. Some will improve and some will worsen. What a company seeks is an overall set of trade-offs which are better for the business as a whole.

Batch-related developments and hybrids

Numerical control machines
An NC system describes a process which automatically performs the required operations according to a detailed set of coded instructions. As mathematical information is the base used, the system is called numerical control. The first applications involved metal-cutting processes such as milling, boring, grinding and sawing but more recently the range of NC applications includes tube bending, shearing and different forms of cutting. Compared with conventional equipment, NC machines offer increased accuracy, consistency and flexibility even with the need to meet very complex manufacturing requirements. Thus, design changes and modifications require only a change in instruction, nothing more.

However, the trade-off against conventional plant is the increased investment associated with NC processes. In addition, it brings with it changes for the operators, setter and supervisor in terms of their role, the level of specialist support and skill requirements, together with the problems involved in the introduction of new technology and associated changes.

In reality, an NC machine is a development of a batch process and one which is low-volume in nature. It is batch because the machine stops at the end of one operation and then either the piece being machined or tool being used to complete the operation (or both) is repositioned or changed. Thus, several set-ups take place within a given program. Similarly, at the end of the program the process is reset for a new job with a new program being loaded. It is low-volume because the set-up times are short, hence providing an acceptable ratio between set-up times and the length of the run time before the next set-up. The position of NC machines on Figure 4.4 illustrates this.

Machining centres
Machining centres, which first appeared in the late 1950s, combine NC operations previously provided by different machines into one

arrangement. With tool changing automatically controlled by instructions on the tape, and carousels holding 150 tools or more, the
underlying rationale for this development is to maximize the
combination of operations completed at a single location. A machining centre typically embraces several metal-cutting facilities (for
example, milling, boring and drilling) which are applied to a given
piece of work in a predetermined sequence which the NC program reflects. Storing the relevant range of tools in the form of a
magazine, the appropriate tool is then selected and the particular
operation completed. The hybrid nature of this process is that
several operations are completed before the item of work is
removed. Thus, a machining centre completes many operations in
sequence and without removing the items from the process. This
reflects aspects of line processing within what is still a batch process
(the process stops and resets itself not only between operations but
between one item and the next).

Flexible manufacturing systems
Whereas a machining centre is best suited to low volume, a flexible
manufacturing system (FMS) is appropriate for mid-volume requirements, as shown in Figure 4.4. This, too, is designed to complete a
given number of operations on an item before it leaves the system.
However, rather than the item being contained in a single centre, in
an FMS the workpiece is transferred from one process to the next
automatically. Besides volume differences, the physical dimensions
of the items to be machined are typically much larger than those
completed by machining centres.

Flexible manufacturing systems are a combination of standard and
special NC machines, automated materials handling and computer
control in the form of direct numerical control (DNC) for the
purposes of extending the benefits of NC to mid-volume manufacturing situations.[4] Whereas NC equipment and particularly machining centres cater for relatively low-volume demand, much less
attention has been given to improving manufacturing's approach to
mid-volume, mid-variety products, although this accounts for a
large part of the products which would fall into the batch range of
volumes.

A typical series of events in processing a part in FMS is as follows:

• A DNC system directs a cart carrying an empty fixture to a load
station and also advises the loader which part is to be loaded.

- On completion the loader signals that it is now ready and the computer directs the part to the first operation, selecting, if available, the lowest backlog potential.

- The part is automatically unloaded, the appropriate NC program selected and the work completed.

- This procedure will be followed until the part is finished whereupon it goes to the unloading area and out of the system.

The hybrid nature of FMS is based on similar logic to that described in the section on machining centres, that is, maximizing the combination of operations completed at a single location. The additional capital investment will bring with it both lower cost and lower work-in-progress inventory advantages, combinations of trade-offs more akin to line processing. However, the root process (see earlier) is still batch.

Group technology
The first three hybrid processes concerned the use of NC equipment as the basis for the process change. However, there are alternative hybrid processes which can be adopted using conventional or non-NC equipment. Three are described here. The first concerns a batch/line hybrid known as group technology.

The underlying difference between the choice of batch and line processes is one of associated volumes. What group technology does is to gain for batch processes some of the advantages inherent in high-volume line situations. It does this by changing the process or functional layout associated with batch manufacturing into the product layout associated with line (see Figure 4.5).

The approach adopted is to separate out those processes which do not lend themselves to the application of group technology due to factors such as the level of investment involved and health considerations (such as noise or process waste/fumes). The next step is to group together families of like products in terms of the processes required.

The third step is to determine the process configuration necessary to manufacture each product family involved and to lay out the cell or line to reflect the manufacturing routings involved. The final stage is to complete a tooling analysis within each family, with a twofold aim. The first is to group together those parts within the family which can use the same tooling. This then forms the basis for scheduling in order to reduce set-up time. The second is to include this feature as part of the design prerequisites for future products.[5]

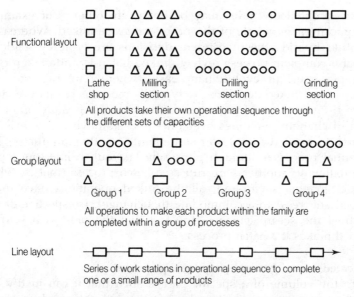

All products take their own operational sequence through the different sets of capacities

All operations to make each product within the family are completed within a group of processes

Series of work stations in operational sequence to complete one or a small range of products

Source: Hill, op. cit., 1991, p. 141 (with permission).

Figure 4.5 Group layout, its relationship to functional (batch) and line (product) layouts to illustrate the transition from the former to the latter

The implications of group technology for a business are that the enhanced volumes have moved the point on the horizontal axis in Figure 4.4 towards the higher-volume end. In so doing, the process choice of group technology substitutes the point on many of the Table 4.1 dimensions associated with a batch process, to that of line. Most importantly, it creates an inherently less flexible process in that to reuse any spare capacity brought about by a decrease in product family volumes will not be easy or even possible without moving the location of the plant, itself a form of process investment. The key advantages to be gained from group technology include reduced lead times and lower work-in-progress inventory, together with a series of advantages associated with any form of small-scale manufacturing unit.

Linked batch
As with most of the developments discussed in this section, linked batch is a hybrid of batch and line. However, linked batch does not need to encompass a large number of processes (which is more typical in the examples given earlier). In some instances, only two or

three sequential processes may be linked, in others (for example, food packing) the whole of the process may be linked. Whereas in the other hybrids the investment decisions are typically made as part of a complete process review, linked batch is undertaken on a more piecemeal or evolutionary basis (where only two or three processes are linked decisions are typically piecemeal in nature, and, where the whole set of processes are linked, this is quite often the result of changing volumes over time and adaptive use of existing capacity to meet the process requirements of other products). The sequential processes, though physically laid out in line (one operation following another), are run as a batch process (that is, when product change is required, all the linked operations have to be stopped and reset to accommodate this change). Irrespective of the length of the set-up changes, the fact that the process has to be stopped makes it a batch process.

Dedicated use of general-purpose equipment

Where the volume of a specific part is such that it can justify the allocation of a process to its sole use, then operations does so. In this instance the dedication is not in the equipment itself but in the use of a general-purpose process. Thus, the potential flexibility and other characteristics illustrated in Table 4.1 of a general-purpose process are still retained and when volumes reduce will be re-claimed.

It will be deduced from this description that characteristically the process is not altered. Hence, the process is still batch and, therefore, general-purpose in nature. What becomes dedicated is the use of the process, which reflects the volume requirements for the product in question.

Line-related developments and hybrids

Just as the last section related to developments and hybrids based on batch processes and which had continued to have their 'root' in that process, so this section reviews hybrids related to line.

Mix mode assembly lines

By investing in order to broaden the range of products with which a line process can cope without stopping, companies purposefully move towards what is known as a mix mode assembly line. In reality, the product range for all line processes is determined at the time of the process investment. However, the term 'mix mode' has been used to reflect processes where systematic and purposeful investment has been made to increase the product range accommodated by the process, whilst typically programming the line to make small quantities of different products in a predetermined sequence. As will have been deduced from this explanation, a mix mode assembly line is not technically a hybrid, in that the characteristics of another process have not been combined with those of line. It is in fact a line process which can accommodate the requirements of a wider range of products than can typically be made on a classic line process. It has been included here to illustrate how process investment can change certain relevant trade-offs in a business.

Transfer lines
The last hybrid process to be discussed is transfer lines. Where the volume demand for products is very high, further investment is justified. Transfer lines are a hybrid between line and continuous processing. However, the root process is still line because it can be stopped without major cost being involved.

The position of transfer lines on Figure 4.4 illustrates the features involved in this process where the high demand justifies investment designed to reduce the manual inputs associated with a line process and move more towards a process which not only automatically moves a part from one station to the next but also automatically positions, completes the task and checks the quality as an in-built part of the process. Furthermore, deviations from the specified tolerances will be registered and automatic tooling adjustments and replacements will often be part of the procedure involved. In order to achieve this, the process is numerically controlled in part or in full, which provides the systems control afforded, at least in part, by the operator in the process.

Product/service profiling

An organization needs to have a comprehensive understanding of the changing implications for its business as different processes are chosen. The earlier sections in this chapter provide these insights.

However, when companies invest in processes they often fail to incorporate these business trade-offs (and subsequent implications) into that decision. Similarly, as markets change they fail to recognize that the trade-offs embodied in their current processes are fixed and will remain so unless further investment is made (in new processes or modifications to existing ones) or unless the corporate expectations of the extent of one or more trade-offs are changed. The former will provide a new set of trade-offs whilst the latter will enable other trade-offs, relating to other aspects of the business, to be achieved. An example of these alternatives is where a business, in order to help achieve lower inventory levels, invests to reduce set-up/make-ready times (the former) or forgoes high machine utilization (the latter).

The concept of product/service profiling offers an organization the opportunity to test the current or anticipated degree of fit between the characteristics of its market(s) and the characteristics of its existing or proposed processes and infrastructure investments. The principal purpose of this assessment is to provide a method to evaluate and, where necessary, improve the degree of fit between the way in which a company wins orders in its markets and the operation function's ability to support these criteria.

In many instances, though, companies will be unable or unwilling to provide the degree of fit desired due to the level of investment, executive energy and time-scales involved. But sound strategy concerns not getting the answers right but improving the level of consciousness an organization brings to bear on its corporate decisions. In such circumstances product profiling will increase corporate awareness and allow conscious choice between alternatives.

Inconsistency between the market and an organization's process/infrastructure capability in terms of supporting the business specification of its product/services, can be induced by changes in the market or process investments, or a combination of the two. In all instances, the mismatch is created by the fact that investments within production/operations are both large and fixed in nature. On the other hand, corporate marketing decisions can often be relatively transient in nature. Whilst this allows for change and repositioning, production/operations decisions bind the business for years ahead. Thus, linkage between these two parts of an organization is not just a felt need but a pragmatic necessity.

Procedure

The procedure adopted in product/service profiling is as follows:

1. Select relevant aspects of products/services, operations, and infrastructure, as outlined in Table 4.1. The key at this stage is

to base the selection of characteristics on their relevance to the particular organizational issues – listing all the dimensions given in Table 4.1 will blur the essential core of the exercise and must be avoided.

2. Display the characteristics of process choice that would be typical for each chosen dimension (as illustrated in Table 4.1).[6] This provides a statement of the dimensions that would typically be expected for each characteristic and thus creates a backcloth against which the product(s)/service(s) are profiled.

3. Profile the product(s)/service(s) by positioning it (them) on each of the characteristics selected. This tests the level of correlation between the market needs and operations management's current or proposed response to the provision of those needs.

4. The resulting profile illustrates the degree of consistency between the characteristics of the market and the business specification of the process and chosen features of investment and infrastructure. The higher the level of consistency, the straighter the profile will be. Inconsistencies will be shown by the dog-leg shape of a profile.

Product/service profiling, therefore, is a way of illustrating the level of fit that exists within an organization or the level that it anticipates as a result of marketing or process/infrastructure investments or as a combination of the two. Figure 4.6 provides one illustration of the use to which product/service profiling can be put. It should be noted that organizations often have several processes within the operations function and each may require to be analyzed separately. The example in Figure 4.6, however, concerns one part (albeit the core) of the manufacturing processes in the relevant company. Each organization will require its own approach and resolution. The example described met the specific needs of the business to which it relates. In no way, therefore, is it intended that the approach illustrated in Figure 4.6 should be considered universally applicable. However, it is the conceptual base on which the analyses rest that can be transferred and used to provide similar insights, where appropriate.

Faced with a decline in markets and profits, the company illustrated in Figure 4.6 undertook a major internal review concerning its two manufacturing plants. To provide orientation to its business it decided to manufacture different products at each of its two sites. This decision resulted in a distinct orientation in each plant in terms of products and associated volumes. Four or five

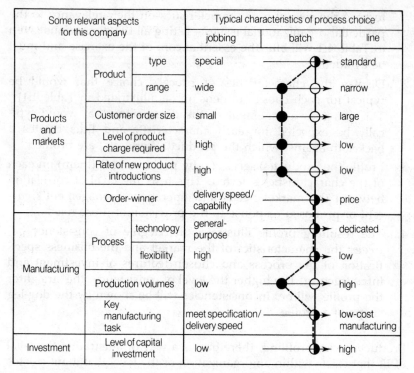

Some relevant aspects for this company			Typical characteristics of process choice		
			jobbing	batch	line
Products and markets	Product	type	special		standard
		range	wide		narrow
	Customer order size		small		large
	Level of product charge required		high		low
	Rate of new product introductions		high		low
	Order-winner		delivery speed/ capability		price
Manufacturing	Process	technology	general-purpose		dedicated
		flexibility	high		low
	Production volumes		low		high
	Key manufacturing task		meet specification/ delivery speed		low-cost manufacturing
Investment	Level of capital investment		low		high

O ◑ Position of plant A on each of the chosen dimensions and the resulting profile

● ◐ Position of plant B on each of the chosen dimensions and the resulting profile

This figure reflects the consistency of products and processes for plant A, and the inconsistencies for plant B reflected by a straight line and dog-leg shape respectively

Source: Hill, op. cit., 1991, p. 71 (with permission).

Figure 4.6 A profile analysis for two plants of a company illustrating the mismatch between one plant and its market induced by applying the same manufacturing strategy to both plants

years later the number of product types handled by Plant B was eight times as many as Plant A, and, as one would expect, product volume changes were reflected in this decision. Whilst in Plant A, average volumes for individual products rose by 60 per cent, in Plant B they decreased by 40 per cent. In addition, to redress the decline in profits, the company also embarked on major manufacturing investments at each plant, involving identical process investments and infrastructure changes: Figure 4.6 illustrates how these changes fitted Plant A's markets whilst they led to a significant mismatch for Plant B.

The procedure followed is the one given in the previous section. Again, the first step is to choose the characteristics of products markets, manufacturing, investment cost and infrastructure features pertinent to this business. The dimensions selected for these two plants are detailed in Figure 4.6. Then, the characteristics that reflect the change between jobbing, batch and line need to be described. On the one hand, the product range associated with jobbing is wide, and becomes increasingly narrow as it moves through to line. On the other, customer order size is small in jobbing and becomes increasingly large as it moves through to line, and so on. These dimensions represent the classic characteristics of the trade-offs embodied in process choice. Plant A's profile shows a straight-line relationship between the products/markets and the manufacturing and infrastructure provision. However, when the profile is drawn from Plant B it can be seen that a dog-leg occurs because the process and infrastructure investments made in that plant, although similar to those made in Plant A, did not relate to the characteristics of its particular market and hence a mismatch occurred.

Issues in service delivery systems

Although the issues dealt with so far have related to the provision of both goods and services, this section is orientated towards issues particular to service delivery systems.

Developing a service specification

By their very nature, services are less tangible than products. Thus, whilst the physical dimensions of a product require specification, services lack these characteristics and hence are intrinsically less defined. The task of undertaking the specification for a service is one, therefore, which an organization must ensure takes place.

Level of server discretion

In manufacturing, customers are invariably separated from the production system through, for example, inventory and the wholesale/retail system. In a service/delivery system the provider and customer are invariably linked at the point of provision. The result is that the provider has the opportunity to interpret what is meant by service within the delivery system. Whilst at the jobbing end of the process continuum server interpretation would be recognized as an integral part of the total process, fixing[7] the specification is an essential task as an organization moves towards line.

Establishing the level of contact with a customer

Deciding the extent of customer participation in a service affects many factors including capacity provision, service levels and costs. Many service industries are increasingly using a higher level of customer involvement in the delivery system including the following:

1. *Supermarkets:* these control over 80 per cent of the gross retail market and sell principally on a self-service basis.
2. *Fast-food outlets:* these form a growing part of overall restaurant provision.
3. *Telephone services:* the introduction of subscriber dialling has led to the majority of telephone calls being made by the customer.
4. *Garages:* self-service petrol provision is now the norm as well as screen washing and oil, water and tyre pressure checks.
5. *Catalogue showrooms:* these are a rapidly growing sector of the retail industry. They require the customer to complete the selection and application part of the procedure, with the business providing a fast delivery service once the transaction is fed into the service system.

The reasons for the growth in these factors vary. Table 4.2 summarizes some of the relevant factors.

Off-line versus on-line

Some services are inherently on-line and do not allow the server to be separated from the customer (for example, hairdressing and passenger transport). However, other service businesses do. Where this is so an important decision is whether some parts of a service should be provided off-line. In addition, once parts of a service are

Table 4.2 Factors for success embracing products and services brought about by do-it-yourself approaches in selected service sectors

Factors for success	Selected service sectors				
	Supermarkets	Fast-food outlets	Telephone services	Garages	Catalogue showrooms
Faster service	√	√	√	√	√
Lower price	√	√	√	√	√
Improved product quality	√	√			
Increased product variety	√				√

Source: Terry Hill, op. cit., 1991, p. 107 (with permission).

provided off-line then it can also be switched from a front office to back-room provision.

The Royal Bank (Canada), for instance, believes that customers' perceptions are a critical factor in service provision. The bank considers that when queues form, customers' attitudes to waiting are affected by the server's attitude when they are eventually attended to, and the fact that, when waiting, customers judge service by the level of attendance shown in the front office. Thus, if bank staff are doing jobs other than attending to customers, and the queues are long, customers' attitudes to the bank's overall regard for service quality are affected. Thus, the bank's aim is to transfer as much paperwork to head office or to the back room as possible.

Capacity decisions

Linked to decisions concerning processes are those involving capacity. This is a critical aspect of operations management due to the constraints it may impose on other planning activities. The objective of capacity is to match the level of operations to that of demand. What makes the task difficult is the uncertainty of demand in terms of overall size and format.

The basic procedure is overviewed in Figure 4.7. This details the steps involved, which are now discussed.

Forecast demand for products/services

Demand forecasting is difficult. No matter which method is used, it will not be accurate. But when planning ahead, coping with inaccuracy is better than having no forecast at all.

A prerequisite for capacity planning is a statement of demand. Businesses making a standard product may need (or decide) to make ahead of demand through the use of finished goods inventory. Other businesses may make components and/or subassemblies in line with forecasts and then assemble to order. Lastly, businesses making to order (which includes most service industries) will only be able to make products or provide services after receipt of an order and hence use the principle of order backlog or forward load as a way of balancing changes in demand to available capacity.

All businesses have planning horizons which differ depending upon lead times. Where the key capacity dimension is labour (as in jobbing and many service industries) the relevant time horizon will be shorter than where the investment is in plant and equipment.

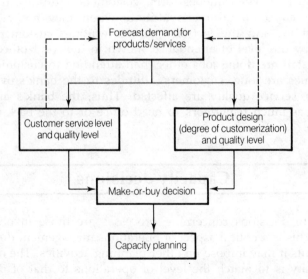

Source: Hill, op. cit., 1991, p. 127 (with permission).

Figure 4.7 Capacity planning procedure for a manufacturing or service business

Product/service design, service and quality levels

Part of the forecasting procedure includes agreement of product/ service specifications and the level of service and quality to be provided. As Figure 4.7 illustrates, these are a separate stage in the procedure but, in fact, feed back into the forecast task. Issues concerning standards, specials and customized products/services and decisions concerning customer investment in the service delivery system have already been addressed. Also in Chapter 3 value engineering and value analysis approaches were explained and their important role in the design process was highlighted (pp. 33–4).

Make-or-buy decision

Theoretically, every item, process or service currently purchased outside could be made inside and vice versa. In reality, however, the choice is not so extensive, but make-or-buy decisions are often not taken with sufficient forethought. Such decisions need to address the strategic and tactical elements involved.

Strategic aspects

- In the pursuit of short-term improvements many organizations have decided to sub-contract tasks traditionally completed in-house. In some instances this may make sense. However, there is a need to recognize whether there is an element of complacency involved. Indeed, some companies have painted themselves into the 'hollow-corporation syndrome'[8] with the long-term consequences of eroding the operations base which will make it more difficult to initiate change.

- The choice of process will also impinge on make-or-buy decisions. Companies, unsure of future demands for a product/ service, will often sub-contract initial operations until they have ascertained the volumes involved, thus avoiding potentially inappropriate process or staff investments.

- Companies developing products/services involved in a stepped increase in technology often have to buy the technology in from outside. Future decisions will, therefore, need to decide whether or not to confirm the initial decision which was sound but of an expedient nature.

- Adequate internal capability to complete current tasks may lead to an initial decision which later is not reviewed.

Tactical aspects
Once relevant strategic issues have been concluded, tactical aspects of the problem can then be considered. They include the following:

- the organization's internal capability to complete the task in terms of conformance quality as well as space and other non-technical considerations;
- the position of the item in the total process and the related interdependence involved;
- availability of suitable suppliers;
- comparative costings including a true reflection of overhead costs;
- protection of supply;
- protection of product, process or service ideas;
- avoiding the subjective element of these decisions (for instance, the belief that no one can do the task as well).

Capacity planning

Capacity concerns the provision of labour, equipment or both to meet the demands for products/services. This will have a time-scale factor in terms of planning horizons and will use, where possible, inventory as a way of transferring capacity from one time period to be sold in the next.

The approach to managing the details of capacity planning is addressed in the next chapter.

Service issues
Some issues which relate more to service delivery systems than to manufacturing have been mentioned already. A summary of these and other capacity-related issues is now provided.

Level of customer involvement
Because of the inherent process/consumer interaction within the service delivery system, the consumer becomes a potential source of capacity. The extent of this involvement is important in terms of the overall source of capacity provision for the following reasons:

1. It has an impact on costs.

2. It affects the provision of capacity at peak points in the service delivery system where all or part of a service is consumed. For example, in a self-service restaurant the role of the waiter is provided partly by the customer.

3. It allows service definitions to be refined with the customer.

4. It provides an opportunity to personalize the process and will thereby influence customer selection.

Demand/capacity imbalance
As service capacity is perishable, a major task concerns adjusting capacity provision and/or attempting to modify demand in an attempt to balance the two. Factors affecting this include the following:

Back room versus front office   Tasks which do not involve customer interface with the server can be provided in the back room. This decoupling allows work to be completed independently of provision and, therefore, lends itself more to cumulating volumes, with attendant gains in efficiency, and facilitates the scheduling of work. For example, part of the Trustee Savings Bank Group's £200 million cost-cutting initiative undertaken in the early 1990s was to close all the back-room activities in its branches and move them to eighty customer service centres. This restructuring illustrated the Group's recognition of the opportunities available in different parts of its service delivery systems.[9]

The front office involves immediate customer response and so requires different responses to those available in the back room. These take two basic forms:

1. Long-term: concerns developing complementary services to help even out demand, including cross-training, thereby allowing greater staff flexibility and the transfer of work from the back room to the front office.

2. Short-term: where demand may be temporarily higher than capacity, layout changes can be used to even out the queuing which would inevitably result – for example, single queues feeding several outlets or the dispensing of numbered tickets to allow customers to 'queue' in a more relaxed manner.

Overbooking capacity   The perishable nature of service capacity has led some organizations to overbook on purpose in order to ensure that the capacity is used as much as possible. The classic example is the airlines. British Airways experience an average 15–25 per cent no-shows and so, like others, overbook in order to keep payloads as high as possible. In 1989, BA admits that it 'bumped' some 10,000 passengers (including volunteers) out of the 23 million it carried.[10]

Location

Normally, either the consumer travels to the service or the service moves to the customer. Some services travel both ways, for example an at-home hairdressing service, and institution-based and distance-learning education. The necessity of bringing together the consumer and provider results in a facility serving a small geographical area. Thus, the location of the facility with respect to its market is critical to success.

Layout

Layout changes in shops and other retail outlets alter the nature of the back-room and front-office provision. Figure 4.8 illustrates a typical change in the Solihull Branch of the Cheltenham and Gloucester Building Society. This creates a system which lends itself to being more approachable and responsive and more akin to the changing image of financial institutions. Also, these types of rearrangement have an impact on the level of customer involvement, demand changes to back-room/front-office arrangements and affect the nature and extent of capacity requirements.

Bottlenecks

As most organizations use batch processes (see pp. 43–4), the recognition of and subsequent analyses associated with bottlenecks are prime tasks in operations.

A bottleneck is a capacity-related phenomenon. It implies that one or more processes/categories of staff have less available capacity than the other processes/categories of staff, just as the neck of a bottle has a lower level of capacity than its body.

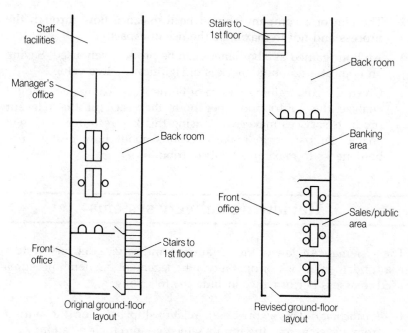

Original ground-floor layout

Revised ground-floor layout

Source: Hill, op. cit., 1991, p. 152 (with permission).

Figure 4.8 The Cheltenham and Gloucester Building Society's Solihull offices (not to scale)

Thus, issues such as material shortages and process breakdowns are important in themselves but are not bottlenecks. Furthermore, where a capacity shortage in a given period can be eliminated by rescheduling work to one or more periods before or after the period in question, this would not be classed as a bottleneck. The origins of such a problem lie in scheduling. Bottlenecks, therefore, imply that the capacity shortage is a permanent and not a temporary phenomenon.

As the definition implies, bottlenecks restrict total throughput. Analyses and approaches concerning bottlenecks reflect this factor, as highlighted below.

1. Bottlenecks are the limiting factor governing the level of work through the total operations processes.
2. The level of utilization of a non-bottleneck is determined not by its own potential but by some other constraint.

3. The aim of a company should be to balance flow through the process and not to maximize the use of capacity.

4. An hour gained at a bottleneck can be productively used. Saving an hour at a non-bottleneck is of significantly less value.

5. Given the constraining nature of bottlenecks, companies should analyze the contribution per hour that each of the relevant products/services make when using this key resource. This will enable companies to make decisions about how best to use bottlenecks to maximize total contribution.

Reviewing delivery systems

The systematic review of the production and service delivery system is a fundamental task of operations management. General measures used to assess performance include the following:

1. *Productivity.* This expresses a relationship between the output from a system and the inputs which go into their creation:

$$\text{Productivity} = \frac{\text{Output}}{\text{Input}}$$

Improvements in productivity can be achieved through favourably altering either the numerator or denominator, or both.

2. *Effective performance.* How well a function performs is calculated as follows:

$$\text{Effective performance (\%)} = \frac{\text{Standard hours of work produced}}{\text{Actual hours worked}} \times 100$$

This measures the amount of work produced compared to the hours worked and thereby expresses the level of performance achieved.

3. *Efficiency.* The final perspective on how well input resources have been used is gained through the efficiency index:

$$\text{Efficiency} = \frac{\text{Actual output}}{\text{Budgeted/expected output}}$$

This compares actual hours produced (output) with the budgeted level of output which would form the basis for cost, capacity and similar calculations.

The aim in most organizations is to improve overall performance and there are three basic levels at which these improvements can be made:

1. scientific – research activities which result in new knowledge;
2. technical – the adoption or application of existing scientific knowledge to replace existing methods;
3. operational – to improve the use of technical developments.

These approaches require different levels of investment, will potentially yield different levels of improvement and will bear fruit over different time-scales. Companies most frequently work at the operational level as their principal approach to gaining improvements.

Operational approaches to improving the delivery system

Many approaches which can be used to improve the existing system have been developed. This section highlights some of the more important ones.

1. *Method study*. This entails the systematic and critical examination of the ways that things are done in order to make improvements.[11] The approaches used have been developed over many decades and the systematic recording and examining of existing methods is followed by developing improved approaches and their installation supported by relevant training.[12]
    Charting techniques and/or video are used to record existing methods in order to enable a systematic analysis to be undertaken.
2. *Set-up reductions*. Technically part of method study, set-up reductions relate to a specific aspect of method improvements which concerns the time taken to complete a change from one

job to the next.[13] In today's markets of declining volumes and wide choice, the need to reduce set-ups has been brought to the fore.

3. *Continuous improvements.* Whereas in the past improving existing methods and procedures was considered to be within the mandate of management, many companies have moved towards involving and empowering people at all levels in the organization to effect change. Only in this way will they be able to move towards a situation where improvement is completed on a continuous basis by those involved in doing the task supported by appropriate training and, where required, by technical support.

Key areas of improvement include the following:

1. *Eliminating waste.* Excesses in all forms are unnecessary and costly, thus a key task is eliminating waste in all its forms. F. Cho (Toyota Motor Company) provides a concise definition of waste as 'anything other than the minimum amount of equipment, materials, parts and workers which are absolutely essential to production'.

2. *Jidoka – quality at source.* Jidoka is based on the philosophy that all individuals must be responsible for the products they make or services they provide. In some manufacturing systems this takes the form of empowering anyone to stop the production system for reasons of quality, safety or pace of the process. With the system at a standstill, all attention is given to resolving the problem.

   The integral nature of provision and delivery in a service system has maintained this essential link within this sector. Ensuring that this is an integral part of service provision, however, is a core task within operations management.

3. *Involving people.* To support these approaches companies need to involve people both within and outside the organization. To accomplish this, work needs to be structured in terms of increased participation, involvement, responsibility/authority links and job interest. This, in turn, leads to a situation where continuous improvement can flourish and where it becomes an integral part of the way an organization works.

   The opportunities and benefits from adopting the hiring-head-as-well-as-hands philosophy present an overwhelming argument. Work-sharing and other part-time employment policies more typical of service businesses place even greater need for involvement if corporate goals of quality, cost and meeting customer needs are to be maintained, let alone improved. Similarly, though often overlooked, the recognition of supplier networks as part of the total service delivery system needs to be made and comprehensively developed as part of the total product/service provision.

Key points review

Companies can theoretically choose any of the processes to complete the task. In reality, there are physical restrictions such as those described on pp. 44–6, but the more fundamental reason why one process is chosen instead of another is to achieve market fit.

To help clarify key differences between processes, a summary of the distinctive features of each is now provided.

- *Project* – used for one-off products/services which have to be built or provided on site because it is difficult or impossible to move them once they have been made. Consequently, and unlike any other process, the resources involved have to be brought to the site and released for reuse elsewhere when they are no longer needed. The building and dismantling features of the process incur significant additional costs.

- *Jobbing* – used for one-off (unique) products/services which do not have to be built/provided on site. As the product/service will not be repeated, investment in the task will be kept to a minimum as it will not be reused. Skilled staff are essential and it is they who carry forward their experience of coping with one-off requirements to the next job.

- *Batch* – with an increase in volume (and normally repetition) companies select batch processes. This justifies investment in all its forms, from engineering/specialist time to decide how best to make the product/provide the service through to investment in terms of equipment and other forms of support.

  To complete the task the first step is set up and the operation(s) completed at this stage. The next part of the process is then set up so that the second operation(s) can be completed, and so on. At each stage the process in question will be set up to complete the required operation and then reset to complete an operation on the next product/service. Thus, to complete another product/service a process (or person) has to be set up to complete each operation in question.

• *Line* – when demand is sufficiently high to justify dedicating equipment solely to making/providing a specified range of products/services, a line process is normally chosen. As a line is designed to handle all products/services allocated to it there is no need for set-ups. To the line, all products/services are the same.

• *Continuous processing* – with even higher demand, and given the constraints explained earlier, further investment is justified. The distinguishing features between line and continuous processing are that whereas in the former operators directly contribute to the making of a product/service and there is no significant cost incurred in stopping and restarting the process, in the latter the process controls itself and the costs of stopping and restarting are prohibitive.

Once processes have been chosen an essential operations task is to review and improve the chosen investments in line with the changing needs of relevant markets.

Many companies develop or invest in hybrids which mix the characteristics of two processes in order to secure a more favourable set of trade-offs from the resulting process configuration. Assessing and monitoring fit between markets and processes and infrastructure provision is a key operations management task and product/ service profiling enables this to be undertaken.

Improving processes and delivery systems is at the heart of the operations task. Approaches and responsibilities are continuously being reassessed and the task of operations management is to keep abreast of developments, and push responsibility for these tasks down the organization so that continuous improvement can be achieved and maintained.

Notes

---

1. There are many additional issues some of which are illustrated and discussed in Terry Hill, *Production/Operations Management: Text and cases* (2nd edn), Prentice Hall International, Hemel Hempstead, 1991, pp. 61–9.

2. NC refers to the operation of machine tools from numerical data stored on paper or magnetic tape, punched cards, computer memory or from direct information. The development of machining centres resulted from the concepts of NC. In a machining centre, a range of operations is provided. The program selects as required from a carousel with up to 150 or more tools (embodied in the centre). Consequently, a machining centre is able to cope not only with a wide range of product requirements but it can also be scheduled to complete one-offs in any sequence desired.

   More advanced NC systems were introduced in the late 1960s in the form of computer numerical control (CNC) which replaced the hard-wired control unit of the NC system with a stored program using a dedicated mini-computer. Hence, the memory storage rather than paper-tape input makes the process more reliable and more flexible in terms of program changes. Also developed were direct numerical control (DNC) systems, in which the computer controls more than one machine tool. A DNC system includes both the hardware and software required to drive more than one NC machine simultaneously. To do this, DNC uses a computer which may be a mini-computer, several microcomputers linked together, a mini-computer linked to a mainframe computer or a mainframe computer on its own.

   A DNC system consists of a number of pieces of NC and/or CNC equipment connected to a centralized computer. The centralized source of information provided by DNC helps in the control of manufacturing. Flexible manufacturing systems (FMS) combine the DNC principle with the other features described in the relevant section on pp. 55–6.

3. In reality, some customization may be offered but the substance of this equipment is standard.

4. P. R. Hass, 'Flexible Manufacturing Systems: A solution for the mid-volume, mid-variety parts manufacturing', SME Technical Conference, Detroit, April 1973; and J. J. Hughes, V. Bagnoll, M. Dooner, J. Hughes, C. Pym and S. Stone, 'Flexible Manufacturing Systems for Improved Mid-volume Productivity', *Proceedings of the Third Annual AIEE Systems Engineering Conference*, November 1975.

5. A fuller explanation is given in Hill, op. cit., 1991, pp. 140–5; also refer to G. A. B. Edwards, *Readings in Group Technology*, Machinery Publishing Company Ltd, 1971, and J. L. Burbidge, *The Introduction of Group Technology*, Heinemann, London, 1975.

6. There are many more dimensions which may be considered than those given in Table 4.1.

7. Note: the difference between personalizing a service and a special/standard service is similar to that described in an earlier section pp. 42–3. Providing customer attention should be part of both a special and standard service. Thus, personalizing a service is an integral part of the service delivery system. However, what a standard service constitutes (that is, the specification) is determined ahead of time.

8. See, for example, 'The Hollow Corporation', Special Report, *Business Week* (3 March 1986).
9. See D. Lascelles, 'Golden era is withdrawn from banks', *Financial Times* (6 March 1989), p. 10, which looks at the growing competition threatening British banks.
10. See A. McWhirter, 'Feeling the squeeze', *Business Traveller* (February 1990), pp. 16–21.
11. See BS 3138 (1979).
12. An extensive review of method study is given in Hill, op. cit., 1991, pp. 301–24.
13. See Hill, op. cit., 1991, pp. 324–6.

5

Controlling operations

The operations function typically supports many of the order-winners and qualifiers in a company's markets. The level of control exercised within operations will, therefore, be an important factor in this essential provision. This chapter deals with two main areas of control – the production/delivery system and inventory.

As with other investments in operations, the systems and controls developed in these two key areas will be large and fixed. Choosing appropriately, therefore, will have important consequences for how well a company is able to meet the needs of its current and future markets.

Planning and control systems

The task of a business is to sell its goods/services in the marketplace and then provide them through its operations function. To do this it invests in the primary facilities of buildings, processes, people and procedures. The problem facing operations is to use these inputs to meet the needs of the market, on the one hand, and meet its own internal performance targets, on the other. The former is the basis of the sale while the latter underpins the very success of the business.

One basic conflict results from the basic difference between markets, which are unstable, and the operations function, which needs to be kept as stable as possible. Whenever operations is exposed to the instability of markets the result is inefficiency. To cope with these opposing characteristics, organizations invest in a number of ways, some of which are shown in Figure 5.1. This section deals with one of the basic cushioning mechanisms, operations planning and control.

The procedures involved in planning and controlling systems cover a wide time horizon from the strategic to the tactical level of decision-making:

- *Long-term operations planning* is a strategic issue generally looking five or more years ahead. It aims to provide for the long-term capacity requirements and resource allocations to meet future organizational objectives in line with future sales levels, new products/services, technology developments and different markets.

- *Medium-term or aggregate planning* is for periods of up to two years ahead and details how demand will be met from available facilities which are considered, in principle, to be fixed.

- *Short-term operations control* handles the day-to-day activities to ensure customer demand is met and resources are used effectively.

This chapter is concerned with medium- and short-term planning and control and outlines some of the more commonly used systems.

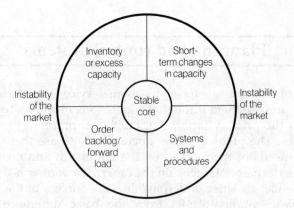

Source: Terry Hill, *Production/Operations Management: Text and cases* (2nd edn), Prentice Hall International, Hemel Hempstead, 1991, p. 195 (with permission).

Figure 5.1 Cushioning the operations core

Aggregate planning

Medium-term or aggregate planning for periods up to two years ahead is used within the overall framework of the long-term plan. How far forward this period extends will reflect the type of business involved and the characteristics of the market it serves. For some firms, therefore, the aggregate planning period will be no more than six months ahead.

It consists of establishing feasible medium-term plans to meet agreed output levels in a situation which is considered relatively fixed. It does this by adjusting demand and capacity variables (workforce levels, overtime, inventory and sub-contracting) within the control of the organization in order to adjust throughput to demand fluctuations.

As sales are received, detailed schedules reflecting the size of the order intake are made and aggregate plans are similarly adjusted up or down. It is at this stage that short-term operations control takes over. Thus, aggregate planning helps to control medium-term changes whilst allowing the short-term fine-tuning of the system to remain within manageable proportions. The steps involved in moving from forecast sales to aggregate plans are now outlined.

1. *Forecast sales.* Initial forecasts are normally adjusted by actual sales trends, thereby hardening the information on future sales patterns.

2. *Make-or-buy decisions.* Make-or-buy decisions reflect the basic in-house provision as well as appropriate supplier capacity.

3. *Select common measures of aggregate demand.* The next step is to aggregate demand for all products/services into statements of common or like capacity groups. For multi-product/multi-service organizations, selecting the common measures needs to be done with care and verified on a regular basis.

4. *Develop aggregate plans.* Set within the context of agreed corporate objectives and operations management's support for the company's markets, aggregate plans are developed based upon the inputs detailed in the first three steps.

5. *Planning horizon.* The development of an aggregate plan has also to be set within an appropriate planning horizon. Typically this will cover several time periods with the plans used on a

month-by-month basis. This reflects the interrelated nature of the operations decisions from one period to the next and recognizes the need for the approach to be able to adjust future decisions with regard to those taken in the past.

6. *Smooth out capacity.* Initial plans will invariably need fine-tuning. One basic task is aligning capacity to sales using a configuration of inventory and changes in capacity. The more common approaches are chase demand, level capacity and a mixed plan.

   Chase demand involves linking demand to throughput rates and capacity. In this way capacity increases and decreases need to be able to be made quickly to respond to changes in sales levels. This has many difficulties and so most companies making standard products use inventory as a way of smoothing demand, as shown in Figure 5.2.

   It is also feasible to choose a mixed plan as a preferred way of coping with the basic task of matching capacity and demand. As shown in Figure 5.3, this uses a combination of inventory and capacity increases to meet forecast sales in different time periods.

   Whereas companies making standard products can avail themselves of inventory-related approaches in resolving these capacity issues, those making special products or providing services cannot make ahead of demand and, therefore, need to choose alternatives.

   (a) *Special products and services.* Companies which make special products or provide special services (especially with a high work content) need to use order backlog/forward load analyses as a principal input into their aggregate plans. Product/service mix trends, and relating these to the capacity requirements of their skilled staff, will also be an important input when assessing future needs.

   (b) *Other services.* Companies which provide 'fast-moving' services (for example, retail outlets and restaurants) will need to analyze product/service mix and demand patterns to establish appropriate capacity requirements. Given the short cycle nature of these businesses, however, aggregate planning will need to reflect known seasonality factors in future capacity provision but most other facets of planning will be closely linked to the short-term control requirements of operations which is dealt with in the next section.

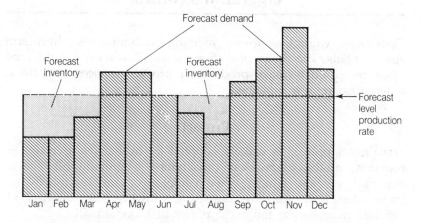

Source: Hill, op. cit., p. 204 (with permission).

Figure 5.2 Level production plan and its effect on capacity

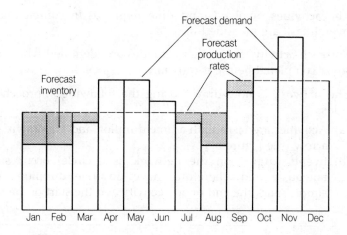

Source: Hill, op. cit., p. 205 (with permission).

Figure 5.3 A mixed plan involving level products, inventory and an increase in capacity from September to December inclusive

Operations control

Operations control concerns meeting a company's short-term specific plans. The choice of system, however, is related to the type of process used to make products or provide services, and these differences are now explained.

Project

The project process is usually adopted by businesses involved in providing products/services of considerable magnitude, often on a one-off basis, and which, when completed, cannot normally be transported. Most tasks are complex and involve many interrelated activities necessitating the development of a formal plan.

The one-off or infrequent nature of these tasks militates against the use of the more traditional scheduling and progressing methods which are described later. To meet the complex, interrelated nature of these types of tasks, companies often use network analysis, the principles of which are now described.

1. The activities involved (and time required) in completing the overall task are identified in detail.

2. For each activity those other activities are identified which need to be completed before it can start.

3. The network is now drawn using the following approach and rules:

    (a) Activities are tasks with a time duration and are drawn as an arrow (see Figure 5.4).

    (b) Events (drawn on the network as a circle) occur simultaneously and, therefore, have no time duration. They simply mark the end of one activity and the start of the next.

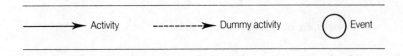

Source: Hill, op. cit., p. 205 (with permission).

Figure 5.4   The symbols used in the drawing of networks

(c) Dummy activities are a convention used in drawing networks and are shown as a dotted arrow (see Figure 5.4).
They enable the network to identify any activity which
depends upon one or more other activities to be completed
before it can start. In this way, therefore, dummy activities
enable the key element of dependency to be shown on a
network which otherwise would make the accurate drawing
of the network diagram difficult or impossible to complete.
(d) Those activities which are not dependent on any other
activity before they can begin will start the network diagram.

The purpose of a network, therefore, is to complete an accurate
representation of the tasks which need to be completed. A network
shows the relevant activities in correct sequence by identifying and
reflecting the dependency of each activity on any one or more other
activities. An activity is said to be *dependent* on one or more activities
if the latter need to be completed before the former can start.

Figure 5.5 provides an example of a completed network. It can be
seen from this that in addition to the activities being drawn in
sequence, the duration of each activity has been given and the
cumulative time taken for each sequence of tasks is also provided. It
will be appreciated that the sequence of tasks the time for which is
the longest will indicate the minimum time in which the whole job
can be completed. This is known as the *critical path* and is marked on
Figure 5.5.

Let us now interpret this network. Events (shown as circles) start
and end an activity. The convention is, therefore, that we start a
network with an event sign and then draw any activity which does
not depend on any other activity being completed before it can start.
In this task there is only one such activity, 'Prepare final drawings'.
So this is drawn and the time duration (5 days) is entered below.
The next event sign shows that this first activity is now complete
and any other activity which depends only on this activity being
completed can now be drawn. In our case this is 'Obtain estimates'.
The event sign at the end of this activity signals it is complete and
therefore any activity depending on the activity 'Obtain estimates'
being completed can now start. In this network the three activities
'Accept quotation and place order', 'Issue materials to sub-contractors' and 'Issue materials internally' can now start. And so on,
through the network.

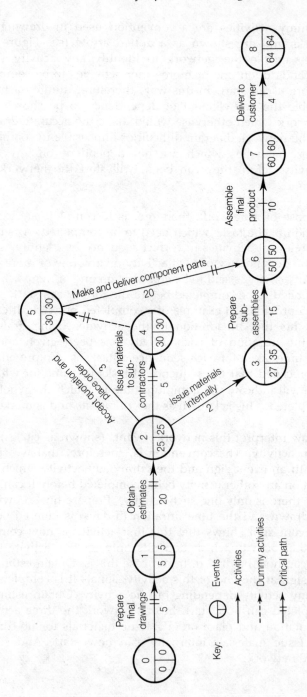

Figure 5.5 Network diagram to represent the activities of a manufacturing task (times in days)

Finally, it will have been noticed that each event sign contains three numbers, as in the following example:

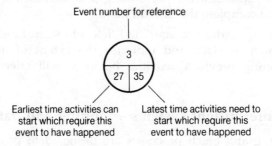

Event number for reference

Earliest time activities can start which require this event to have happened

Latest time activities need to start which require this event to have happened

- Event numbering is for reference purposes only.

- Earliest time activities can start – this is simply the cumulative total of the times to complete all activities leading to this event. In our example, this is

	Days
Prepare final drawings	5
Obtain estimates	20
Issue materials internally	2
Total	27

- Latest time activities need to start – the minimum time needed to complete all the jobs involved is, in fact, the longest path through a network and is known as the 'critical path'. It is important to know this as it signals that delays to any activity on this path will increase the total time taken. The 'latest time' figure signals this and is calculated by subtracting from the total at the end of the diagram (in our case, 64 days) the time taken for each preceding activity. So, to get 35 we subtract the following from 64 days.

	Days
Deliver to customer	4
Assemble final product	10
Prepare sub-assemblies	15
Total	29

These calculations are completed in all instances.

- The critical path is, therefore, the sequence of activities where the 'earliest to start' and 'latest to start' are the same cumulative times. This signals that the activity must be started at the same time it would be available to be started. Thus, any delay on an activity (either finishing or starting) will increase the overall time taken to complete the task on hand.

• Where the 'earliest to start' and 'latest to start' times differ, this is known as slack and indicates the extent of any delay in completing previous activities before it will effect the critical path.

Intermittent systems – jobbing and batch

Both jobbing and batch processes are designed to provide a wide range of products/services in small quantities. They are classified as intermittent because the product/service does not flow through the system but rather goes through a series of stops and starts.

Jobbing
The jobbing process supplies orders which will not be repeated or where the time interval between identical orders will be long. Thus, the situation is a make-to-order provision of goods or services. Also, as products/services are not repeated, investment in the process providing the product/service is not warranted. The experience of handling unique products/services is captured by the skilled staff, who thereby are the principal form of capacity with the equipment involved playing a supporting role.

As the task has not been previously undertaken, an estimate of the time to complete the job is used, and a bar chart similar to that in Figure 5.6 is a typical way of scheduling.

Batch
The short-term control task for a batch process usually concerns the loading, sequencing and scheduling of a wide range of products/ services often involving a large number of operations and using shared staff and equipment. The task is made the more difficult by the varying volumes involved.

The sharing of staff and equipment complicates the control task due to the different orders having different priorities and the impact of this on meeting overall customer delivery dates. Figure 5.7 shows the use of a bar chart to control a relatively simple (in terms of the number of jobs, processes and people involved) set of tasks. It does, however, illustrate the principles involved which would also be the basis of a more complicated set of control requirements.

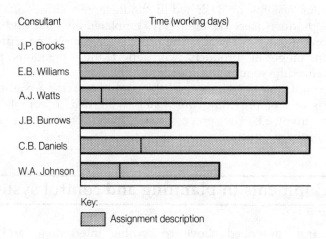

Source: Hill, op. cit., p. 211 (with permission).

Figure 5.6 Bar chart representing assignment allocation to management consultants

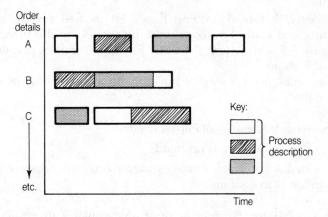

Source: Hill, op. cit., p. 213 (with permission).

Figure 5.7 Orders shown against process sequence on a time scale

Continuous systems – line and continuous processing

Continuous systems are designed to handle large volumes of a small range of products (services are rarely completed on a line and never using continuous processing). The process for completing a product or given range of products will reflect the operations to be completed in the required sequence.

As a result, the key element of the control task for a continuous system is one of providing the materials needed to complete the products involved. The process itself then 'controls' the actual making of the product.

Developments in planning and control systems

The controls described above concerning intermittent and continuous systems outlined the principles involved. To help in this explanation, the examples given also represented smaller and less complex control requirements. However, many companies, particularly those involved in making complex products, use more sophisticated procedures and the most commonly used ones are now described.

However, before describing these, let us first review how the planning and control systems work by discussing the three phases in Figure 5.8 which form the basis for more complex planning and control systems.[1]

Companies need a way of building up a programme of work to ensure that:

- materials become available as needed;
- adequate capability is on hand;
- a schedule of work emerges identifying who does what and when it is to be done.

All this needs to take into account any available inventory in the system and in the context of customers' delivery requirements. In smaller companies, especially where the task is not complex, controls used can be simple in form with much of the detail carried on existing paperwork or in the job knowledge of the people involved. However, in many companies, controls using a combination of procedures, job knowledge and other systems would be inadequate. In these situations firms have to develop a control system, the principles of which will be based on the outline in Figure 5.8.

1. *Front End.*[2] The first task is to translate sales into a statement of demand. The master production schedule (MPS) does this using forecasts, known orders and operations capacity data. This then forms the 'front end' of the system which details what is to be made or provided in future time periods.

2. *Engine.* The aim of any control system is to schedule work in line with customers' delivery requirements. However, there are many steps to be undertaken between demand statements and detailed schedules and these comprise the 'engine' of the system. As Figure 5.8 shows, the steps are as follows:

   (a) Using product/service structure records, the system translates demand into material requirements. These gross needs are then netted down to take account of any inventory on hand or in progress.
   (b) When the net requirements are known, these are translated into material requirements by exploding the bill of material for each item.
   (c) This information is then translated into capacity requirements and order releases.

3. *Back End.* The final output is the shop-floor schedules and documentation involving purchase orders, works orders and reschedule notices.

The basic system, therefore, is a straightforward translation from statements of demand to detailed instructions on what to make and what materials to buy. The three developments outlined below will all need first to generate an MPS. Where the differences occur is in the 'engine' and particularly 'back end' phases of each system.

Material requirements planning

The system known as *material requirements planning* (MRP) looks at future requirements for finished products/services and uses this and other information to generate statements on the subassemblies, components and raw materials necessary to complete the end products. It is often known as a 'push' system (as opposed to a 'pull' system, such as just-in-time, described below) in that statements of

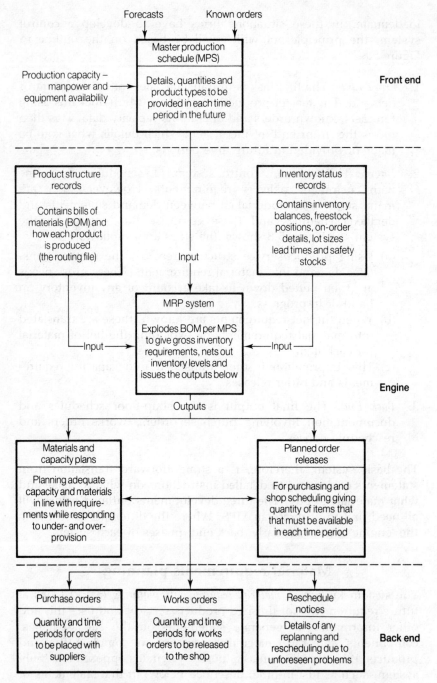

Figure 5.8   Inputs and outputs from a planning and control system

requirements are made in line with agreed delivery dates and schedules created to meet these. In this way the necessary sub-assemblies, components and raw materials are pushed into the process.

MRP is a time-phased, materials-ordering system. Referring back to the basic system described under 'Intermittent systems', the key similarities will be seen. The advent of low-cost computing has enabled these systems to be used in forms where the products are complex and involve many operations. Thus, all the different steps and cross-checks necessary to devise a comprehensive and accurate system to control what is a very complex problem can now be accomplished in terms of running costs and also to meet the time-scales needed to keep the system regularly updated. Before low-cost computing was available, the systems used to control the more complex set of tasks were often a combination of systems supplemented by an expediting system whose role was to identify current requirements and prioritize the behind-schedule parts. Low-cost computing offered companies the opportunity to plan and control the operations function of their complex businesses in an orderly way using MRP principles.

The independent/dependent demand is a basic element of MRP. Products/services with an independent pattern of demand are those which do not depend on the demand for any other. Examples include finished products/services and also components and sub-assemblies to be sold as spares. Demand for independent items is calculated by using known orders or forecasts. This then forms the MPS over one or more time periods.

MRP relies on the fact that the demand for all subassemblies, components and raw materials are dependent upon the demand for the finished products/services. They are said to have *dependent* demand. Thus, a dependent item is one that goes into the manufacture of another item or is converted into a higher-level product. For such items only one forecast is necessary. It must be made at the highest level (that is, where the item has an independent demand pattern) from which all other demands can be calculated. As will be seen, this is how an MRP system works.

Just-in-time

The advent of low-cost computing enabled the widespread use of MRP systems. Compared with the confusion and disorder associated with systems supported by expediting and constantly changing priorities, MRP offers a well-ordered system reducing the need to reschedule frequently. However, an alternative approach is one first developed in the Japanese automobile industry and which has now gained much support in other industrial countries. It is known as the *just-in-time* (JIT) production system. Whereas MRP is a plan-push system, JIT is a demand-pull system (see Figure 5.9).

The JIT production system is relatively simple, requires little use of computers and in some industries can offer far tighter control than computer-based alternatives. The idea is to produce and deliver goods just in time to be sold, subassemblies just in time to be assembled into finished goods, fabricated parts just in time to go into subassemblies and purchased materials just in time to be transformed into fabricated parts.[3] The purpose is for all materials to be in active use within the total process. Thus, JIT is based upon the concept of producing small quantities just in time, in contrast to many current alternatives based on making inventory 'just in case' it is required.

With this continued spread of JIT, many varieties and hybrids have been developed. Unfortunately, many of these purport to be something they are not. This is because those developing these alternatives have not recognized the concepts underpinning JIT and thus have introduced apparent JIT initiatives without recognizing (and consequently explaining to others within the company) the significant differences involved. So what are the key principles? There are two. The first is the development of small factory units, each delivering to one another in successive stages of production and eventually to the assembly plant. The second is that everyone works to a system in which each factory unit schedules to a lead time of one day. What happens is that on one day each unit delivers to the next unit the exact quantity it needs to complete its own schedule on the following day. To do this a uniform daily demand

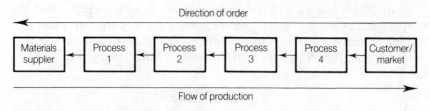

Source: Hill, op. cit., p. 217 (with permission).

Figure 5.9   The flow of orders and operations in a JIT control system

pattern is set throughout the entire system. This means, in turn, that each part of production is developed to handle relatively low volumes (thus, reducing set-up times is a prerequisite for the introduction of JIT), and that the locations of each stage are geographically close to make sense of the logistics.

The concept is very appealing. However, there are several prerequisites if it is to be achieved. First, it is best suited to high-volume manufacturing. Second, it must be end-user driven. The business making the final product has to take responsibility for initiating the development and ensuring liaison with suppliers. Third, schedules must be firm. If the material is not in the system then changes cannot be met. Equally, reducing volumes within the schedule would lead to inventory excesses. Thus, schedule changes can be made only in line with material lead times. Finally, suppliers must be geographically close to customers, thereby enabling regular deliveries to be made. If not, then the element of delivery costs would necessitate more material being delivered than required for one day's production which, in turn, would mean that more than one day's requirement would have had to have been made and so on.

Optimized production technology

Recently, much attention has been given to a proprietary system called *optimized production technology* (OPT). It comprises two parts:

(a) the conceptual base of the system;
(b) the software package (OPT/SERVE) which supports the system.

OPT's main impact concerns shopfloor control (part of the back end of the system).[4] In essence, it is a sophisticated control system based on finite loading procedures and which concentrates on a subset of work centres (the bottlenecks). OPT stresses general fundamental insights which are briefly described here:

1. In any set of resources there will be capacity constraints (or bottlenecks), for some parts of any system will have more capacity than others. The key task is to load the system in line with the capacity of these constraints.

2. Loading the constraints in (1) recognizes that the level of achievable throughput is the factor governing what a company will eventually be able to make and hence sell. The alternative,

adopted by many companies, is to adopt a policy of maximizing resource utilization. But making part products in excess of what can be handled by another part of the system will result only in work-in-progress inventory.

3. Given (1) and (2) above, the bottlenecks govern both throughput and inventory levels in the system. The aim, therefore, is to reduce bottlenecks.

4. Overall, therefore, the aim is to balance flows and not capacity. Reducing bottlenecks by increasing available capacity will increase the flow of the total system, thereby realizing some existing capacity of other processes.

5. The key task then is to reduce bottlenecks in order to increase total throughput. Increasing capacity of a non-bottleneck is of no advantage.

The principles underlying the OPT philosophy have universal applicability. Consequently, they can be used to enhance many existing control systems, as well as helping to improve the effective management of the production/operations function.

Short-term changes to meet demand fluctuations

The previous sections have discussed different approaches to the control of operations and outlined several system developments which companies may use. In addition, companies often seek other ways of meeting changes in demand as another element of their overall approach to this important function.

After future demand has been determined and capacity requirements and their provision have been assessed, companies are able to identify ways of fine-tuning capacity in the short term through bringing about changes in demand and/or capacity. These particular issues are often more pertinent in service than in manufacturing firms because of the very nature of service provision.

Service capacity is perishable and not transferable. Therefore, when demand falls short of capacity, the result is idle capacity. This brings with it a major control problem which is important to the service sector because work content in services cannot be stored, and domestic and social habits create peaks and troughs in service demand (for example, people sleep, eat, work, partake in leisure activities and holiday at similar times).

The result is that balancing demand and capacity is often the more difficult in these circumstances. In addition, before considering short-term ways of meeting these potential imbalances it is important to stress one further point in service provision. Whereas the specification of a manufactured item is well defined, this is not necessarily so in a service package. There is, therefore, an important task of defining customer service and quality levels. Difficulties arise, in part, from the server–customer interface and the potential reshaping of the service specification which may take place as a result.

There are several ways of bringing about short-term changes to this age-old problem of managing demand/capacity imbalances. They include the following:

1. *Re-shaping demand*
   (a) *Changing the pattern of demand* – bringing about changes in demand can be achieved in a number of ways:
      (i) attempting to reduce demand to bring it more in line with capacity (for example, refusing business or increasing overall price levels);
      (ii) changing the pattern of demand (for example, by altering price levels to differentiate between peak and off-peak business and by advertising);
      (iii) introducing products/services with a complementary demand pattern (for example, using hotels for conferences to attract business in off-peak times).
   (b) *Planned and random demand* – in the provision of services, demand can be classified as planned and random. Although the proportion will reflect business differences, the principle behind this separation will help in the overall control task. Once identified, planned demand can be arranged to fill in the troughs as much as possible and so help smooth out the overall demand pattern.
   (c) *Complementary services* – to de-emphasize waiting in the service delivery system, many companies introduce complementary services which can be bought during this period (for example, bar lounges to accommodate customers waiting for a restaurant table).

2. *Changing capacity*

   An alternative to reshaping demand is to change the nature or level of capacity. This can be done in a number of ways:

   (a) *Customer participation* – increasing customer participation in the service delivery system not only contributes to overall capacity provision but also provides capacity at the exact moments it is required, thereby reducing the need to meet these more difficult demand points.

   (b) *Core and secondary capacity* – separating capacity into core and secondary provision enables a company to consider different ways of supplying each of these. Core capacity is geared to meeting the essential or basic needs of the service and is normally highly stable in its provision, whilst secondary capacity is often adjustable, for example through part-time and temporary staff.

   (c) *Flexible capacity* – using flexible capacity can often be a sound way of accommodating demand and service mix changes. Cross-training to enable job changes in peak and non-peak demand times is one example.

   (d) *Short-term capacity adjustments* – transferring staff to another area, using temporary employment, adjusting the length of the working week or repositioning holiday entitlement are examples which companies may consider as appropriate ways of adjusting short-term capacity.

   (e) *Absorbing and releasing capacity* – the use of sub-contracting and the bringing forward/deferment of maintenance schedules are examples of ways in which a company may accommodate an anticipated demand–capacity imbalance.

3. *Scheduling*

   As already described, scheduling helps to accommodate demand fluctuations by spreading demand over time, reducing/ increasing the size of the order backlog or making to stock. In addition, service firms are increasingly using reservation and appointment systems, as explained below:

   (a) *Appointment service* – an appointment service improves control over the timing of arrivals, reduces customer waiting and improves the utilization of capacity.

   (b) *Reservation system* – similarly, a reservation system helps formulate a better estimate of demand and also reduces customer disappointment.

Inventory control systems

Inventory in most businesses is a very large asset. In many manufacturing companies it is the largest asset on the balance sheet and often accounts for in excess of 25 per cent of the asset total.

Approaches in the past to controlling this significant investment were based initially on mathematical formulae which, with the advent of computers, changed to a view that improving systems would lead to improved information which, in turn, would result in better inventory control. However, the fact of the matter is that the key to controlling inventory is knowing why it is there and the function it performs. But before we discuss these approaches in detail, let us establish the relevant context into which these issues need to be placed.

Information on inventory

All companies categorize their inventory holding into three main headings

- raw materials and components;
- work-in-progress;
- finished goods.

The reason for this is that they are legally required to use these categories in their balance sheet. One important side-effect is that this is often the only breakdown of information available. However, upon closer inspection it can be seen that it tells a company little about what is in fact a very large asset. In essence, the information says that the inventory has not been altered (raw materials and components) or it is finished (finished goods) or it is somewhere in between (work-in-progress).

Attitudes towards inventory

Ownership of inventory is a fundamental aspect of its control. Many companies have functionalized their response such that those functions not responsible have been indifferent to their own role and the eventual outcome. In addition, this approach has led to different pressures being applied to reduce inventory which are

Type of inventory	General preference		
	Accounting	Production/ operations	Sales
Raw materials	Low	High	Indifferent
Work-in-progress	Low	High	Indifferent
Finished goods	Low	Indifferent	High

Source: Hill, op. cit., p. 260 (with permission).

Figure 5.10   General preferences of three key functions towards the level of inventory holding

stereotyped in nature rather than based on corporate needs and agreed development (see Figure 5.10).

Size of inventory and basic controls used

As mentioned earlier, inventory is often the largest single asset on a company's balance sheet. As such it is invariably larger than depreciated plant and equipment, and yet corporate controls over these two investments are markedly different.

Many companies use relatively sophisticated investment appraisal systems to help decide whether or not to go ahead with a proposal. However, companies typically do not evaluate inventory investment and usually control it after the event. Where this happens companies demand very rapid inventory reductions. The speed of these demands for improvements, however, is based more on the way in which managers wish to exert control and less on understanding the realistic time-scales involved.

The key to reducing inventory is based on knowing why the current levels exist, changing the rules/procedures which caused this excessive build-up and then, over time, draining off the unwanted inventory whilst only allowing agreed additions to be made.

Inventory levels and control systems

The planning and control systems outlined earlier also impact the level of inventory within a system. Given appropriate business conditions, companies are able to develop JIT applications with the attendant low work-in-progress inventory potential.

Inventory levels and process choice

Expected levels of inventory will also change depending upon the process used by a company to make its products or deliver its services. As Table 5.1 shows, inventory levels can be expected to change depending upon the type of processes used by a firm.

Table 5.1 Relative inventory levels within each type of process

Type of inventory	Type of process				
	Project	Jobbing	Batch	Line	Continuous processing
Raw materials and components	As required	As required	⟶	Planned plus buffer stock	Planned plus buffer stock
Work-in-progress	High	High	Very high	Low	Low
Finished goods	Low	Low	⟶	High	High

The functions provided by inventories

The last section explained that the information on inventory levels which most companies have available is that of raw materials, work-in-progress and finished goods. However, this provides insufficient insights on which to base adequate controls let alone form the basis for continued reduction and fine-tuning of inventory.

The key to understanding inventory and hence knowing sufficient about it to be able to reduce it effectively is to know why it is there. Regardless of their form, inventories may be further described as one or more of decoupling, cycle, pipeline, capacity-related and buffer. Each of these fulfils a specific function, as is now explained.

1. *Decoupling inventory* separates one process from another. In jobbing there is no decoupling inventory as the skilled person will progress a job on a continuous basis. In the same way, there will also be none in line. However, decoupling inventory is a common feature of batch. Inventory in this category decouples one process from the next, allowing them to work independent-

ly and separate what would otherwise be dependent parts of the total operation. The emphasis is on the material waiting for the process (or person) so that the latter can be most efficiently used.

2. *Cycle inventory* relates to the decision to manufacture a quantity of products (sometimes referred to as a lot/batch size) which reflects costs such as set-ups. There is typically no need for this type of inventory in either jobbing or line but it will be a common feature in decisions when using a batch process.

3. *Pipeline inventory* concerns the inventory support necessary when a company decides to sub-contract a process to an outside supplier. Whilst this decision is common with batch and sometimes jobbing processes, it is not so in line/continuous processing.

4. *Capacity-related inventory* refers to the use of inventory to transfer capacity from one time period to the next. It is, therefore, one of the means that companies can use to help smooth out imbalances between capacity and sales levels. Make-to-order situations such as those in jobbing and some batch processes cannot avail themselves of this opportunity. It is possible only where companies make standard products and decide to make them ahead of demand. However, companies making high-volume products often prefer to make these with regard to known orders or schedules (for example, European car makers). In these instances, they are restricted in the use of this form of inventory.

5. *Buffer inventory* concerns the basic problem that demand varies around some average value. Buffer inventory's function, therefore, is to help protect the system against the unpredictable variations in either demand or supply.

Approaches to controlling inventory

This section discusses approaches to help control inventory. They can be used independently of any other initiatives but will always need to recognize the context in which they are to be applied which includes the following:

- the nature of the business, for example make-to-stock or make-to-order customer responses;

- the choice of process and inherent inventory implications;
- the planning and control system used.

Causal analysis

An earlier section (pp. 101–2) expressed the need for inventory to be analyzed in terms of the function(s) it provides or the reasons why it is there. This questioning forms the basis of causal analysis and the procedure to be followed is now explained.

1. The initial step is to select the aspect of inventory (for instance, finished goods) or area/part of the process (a department) which is to be examined. Where this approach is new to the firm, choosing a manageable task has many advantages.

2. The analysis can be completed at any time, but in some instances (such as a work-in-progress check in one of the operations areas) it will need to be done at the end of a working day or week.

3. The inventory is then checked as follows:
   (a) The current position of the inventory in the process is identified.
   (b) A causal check on its function or role is carried out. Where it is considered that a parcel of inventory provides more than one function then a split between the two or more functions is agreed.
   (c) The inventory is evaluated. However, in order to speed up the procedures, in cases of uncertainty an arbitrary figure is agreed.
   (d) Inventory totals are worked out (£s) by position in the process.
   (e) Areas of high inventory are investigated.
   (f) The causes of inventory, once identified, become the priority targets for improving the procedures or changing the rules to prevent an inventory build-up for these reasons.
   (g) Existing inventory is gradually sucked out of the business and overall inventory levels fall as the intake is now tightly controlled and, over time, the excesses are eliminated. Note that in many instances the reduction in inventory will not come by eliminating it totally but by lowering current levels.

Time-scales
Many companies understandably seek inventory reductions in the shortest possible time. However, it is important to be realistic.

Inventory reduction by causal analysis is no quick fix: in a company of medium complexity, 6–9 months may prove to be a realistic time. In a complex organization (for example, making components/subassemblies for the aerospace industry) perhaps twice as long might be needed.

Corporate versus operations inventory

The five functions detailed earlier relate to operations inventory (that is, that which the operations function needs and uses for its own purposes and to help it discharge its various tasks). However, typically some 20–25 per cent of total inventory will be there for non-operations reasons, and this is known as *corporate inventory*. Examples of corporate inventory include the following:

- customer service parts or repair items being held until requested by the customer;
- customer banks – inventory held at a customer's request, normally as a safeguard for that customer's supply;
- safety supplies, resulting from a corporate decision to hold raw materials and component inventory as a safeguard against future supplies;
- credit holds – inventory ready for delivery but held for concerns of customer creditworthiness;
- inventory holdings above the normal level as part of a marketing strategy (for example, promotions);
- that inventory which falls within an organization's definition of 'slow-moving';
- policy inventory – inventory over and above normal levels which has been caused as a direct consequence of a policy decision.

Causal analysis is based on the simple concept that knowing why inventory has been created is the basis for its reduction. It can, as seen by the ideas and details given above, be applied to all forms of inventory and has proved to be an effective way of reducing inventory no matter what basic planning/control and inventory systems are in place.

ABC analysis

Inventory is invariably large in monetary terms. Completing a Pareto analysis of current inventory holdings helps in establishing where to spend time and effort to gain best results. For each item two pieces of information are needed – unit value and annual usage. The product of these two figures is known as the *annual requirement value* (ARV). The inventory items are then placed in descending order of ARV.

The spread of results often reflects what is known as the 80/20 rule – in general it can be said that about 80 per cent of the total ARV will be accounted for by about 20 per cent of the items. This phenomenon is the basis for an ABC analysis, the purpose of which is to separate the different pockets of inventory into high, medium and low holding.

As a guide, a typical split in terms of percentage of parts/items and the corresponding percentage of the total ARV is given in Table 5.2. With these categories a company will then concentrate its control efforts on the high-value items (category A) and thereby achieve the best overall control. Similarly, control over category C items will be broad-brush in nature as the cost of tight controls cannot be justified.

Table 5.2 Typical percentage split in terms of ARV within an ABC analysis

Category	Items	ARV
A	20	80
B	35	15
C	45	5

Key points review

The key topics highlighted in this chapter are now summarized to provide an overview of the issues discussed.

1. *Strategic context.* It is always important to bear in mind the strategic context in which investments in operations processes and infrastructure need to be made. The purpose is to enable a company to manage and control its business so as to meet the needs of the market and make profits today and tomorrow.

2. *Inherent sales/capacity imbalance.* The rate of sales will seldom be in line with the capacity provided inside a company. Companies

seek ways, therefore, of cushioning the operations core from the instability of market demand. Two commonly used approaches are operations control and inventory.

3. *Planning and control systems.* The time phases relating to the planning and control systems will reflect the nature of the business. In general, however, the three levels concern the long, medium and short term. The long-term level is linked to strategic issues such as buying capacity ahead of demand. Medium-term/aggregate planning attempts to overview future needs in order to create a manageable balance between overall demand and capacity. Short-term control then refines capacity in line with what it has been decided to make or provide.

4. *Operations control* will be chosen in line with the type of process used in the production/service delivery system. The broad groupings are
   (a) project;
   (b) intermittent systems (jobbing and batch);
   (c) continuous systems (line and continuous processing).

   Each type will have its own basic system even though the detailed nature of the chosen procedures will need to reflect the complexity and size of the operations control task.

5. *Inventory* is often the largest single asset on a company's balance. The control of this large asset, therefore, is an essential task of operations management.

6. *Inventory control* needs to be a combination of
   (a) choice of process;
   (b) planning and control system;
   (c) causal analysis;
   (d) ABC systems.

Notes

---

1. The three stages in an operations planning control system are described in T. E. Vollman, W. L. Berry and D. C. Whybark, *Manufacturing Planning and Control Systems* (3rd edn), Irwin, Homewood, Ill., 1991.
2. Developed from Terry Hill, *Production/Operations Management: Text and cases* (2nd edn), Prentice Hall International, Hemel Hempstead, 1991, p. 238 (Figure 9B.1).

3. One of the earliest statements providing this definition comes from R. J. Schonberger, *Japanese Manufacturing Techniques: Nine hidden lessons in simplicity*, Free Press, New York, 1982, p. 16.
4. A comprehensive summary of OPT and its contributions to all parts of a planning and control system is provided in Vollman *et al.*, op. cit., pp. 801–13.

6

Quality

Quality has received much attention in the last decade and there has been an increased awareness of its importance in all its many guises. The result has been continued efforts to improve all associated aspects of quality to meet the revised expectations of most customers.

Whilst the word 'quality' attracts immediate attention and brings with it a sense of importance, careless use of the word has created some confusion concerning its meaning. In the sections which follow, some of the key developments are explained which will also help clarify the important differences which exist between the varying facets which the word 'quality' is used to embrace.

Concept of quality

The concept of quality concerns how well and for how long a product/service meets the requirements of the customer. The quality of a product/service is, therefore, the result of two separate activities: product/service design and the operations systems that make the product or provide the service.

The issues around design involve the primary characteristics of performance as well as the dimensions of features and aesthetics and were addressed in Chapter 3. Meeting the specification is the dimension of quality conformance which will be dealt with here in terms of the process and also the approaches and initiatives which are pertinent to that provision.

Quality assurance and quality control

There are two distinct quality functions within the task of making a product or delivering a service. The first is quality assurance. This is concerned with determining the procedures to be used and the type and frequency of checks/tests to be made within the system in order to ensure that the system is meeting the specification embodied in the product/service design.

The second is quality control. This concerns the actual checking or completion of the various tasks involved in the quality procedures which have been determined within the quality assurance function. Whilst the latter is often best completed as a centralized function due to the test equipment investment and/or level of skilled staff required, the former is normally best undertaken within the operations function and at the time the job is completed. Recent developments and the place of quality control within the job of work are addressed in the next chapter.

Developments concerned with quality

Since the late 1970s there has been not only a marked increase in consumer and customer expectations with regard to quality conformance but also a parallel increase in attention by firms in both the industrial and service sectors. The initiatives are now overviewed in terms of the principal national and corporate developments.

National developments

Many governments, increasingly concerned about the erosion of their own manufacturing and associated wealth creation, have introduced standards and initiated activities in areas of quality in order to strengthen their competitive position at home and to enable companies to compete abroad. Some of these are now outlined.

BS 5750
The British Standards Institute (BSI) has been in the product certification business for many years. However, product certification has its limitations, and to meet the expressed needs of industry the BSI introduced in 1979 a System for the Registration of Firms of

Assessed Capability in those situations where product certification is
impractical. The current system is BS 5750 (1987). Where a firm's
design capability is to be included in the assessment, BS 5750 Part 1
is used. Where a firm makes or provides to a published or a
customer's specification, then BS 5750 Part 2 or Part 3 is used.

BS 5750 is a practical national standard for quality systems for use
by companies of all sizes. It identifies the basic disciplines and
specifies the procedures and criteria to ensure that a firm's products/
services meet customers' requirements. It does this by building on
quality at every stage, and sets out how to establish an effective
quality system with appropriate documentation.

BS 5750 comprises nineteen sections. A company which has
completed implementation of these is entitled to appear in the
Department of Trade and Industry's Register on Quality-Assessed
UK Companies. The principal requirements are as follows:

1. *General provisions*
    (a) Good organization – identify and assign responsibility for all
        quality-related functions, with one designated manager with
        sufficient authority to coordinate, monitor and manage the
        quality system.
    (b) Periodic and systematic reviews – internal reviews listing
        defects, problem areas, suggested improvements and a
        record of the corrective action taken.
    (c) Quality system – developed to link with the other relevant
        functions such as design, development, manufacturing,
        sub-contracting and installation.
    (d) Quality planning – identify improvements in areas such as
        testing and inspection.
    (e) Documentation and records – to cover test and measuring
        equipment monitoring.

2. *Specific provisions*
    (a) Design function – to be specified and controlled and com-
        prising a design and development programme to include
        evaluation of new materials, use of value engineering design
        interface, review procedures and appropriate use of data
        feedback from previous designs.
    (b) Evaluation of subcontractors and suppliers – to include
        written documentation, controls and procedures for verifi-
        cation and inspection.

(c) Controlled conditions – all manufacturing operations to be carried out under controlled conditions with appropriate procedures and work instructions on the shop floor.

(d) In-process quality plans – including sampling and rules of acceptance.

(e) Final test – includes procedures, test equipment capability assessment and environmental checks.

Many companies (and increasingly those in the service sector) are now requiring all their suppliers to be BS 5750 registered. Thus, the decision to comply with BS 5750 not only makes sense in itself but also is a prerequisite for entering many markets.

ISO 9000

The ISO 9000 series includes three documents (9001–9003) that define requirements for supplier quality systems. ISO 9001 is the most comprehensive of the three and covers quality assurance and control in design/development, production, installation and servicing. ISO 9002 is for application to production and installation and 9003 to final inspection and test. The coverage is comprehensive and the main sections of ISO 9001 are as follows:

1. Management responsibility – including quality policy, organization and management review.
2. Quality system.
3. Design control – concerning design/development planning and design input, output, verifications and change procedures.
4. Document control – covering approval, issue and modification.
5. Purchasing – assessment of sub-contractors, purchasing data and verification procedures.
6. Product identification and traceability.
7. Inspection and testing – all areas from receiving to in-process and final test, together with records and procedures.
8. Inspection, measuring and test equipment.
9. Quality records and internal quality audits.
10. Training and statistical techniques.

It is intended in future years to replace BS 5750 with ISO 9000 in order to create a common international standard on quality and related procedures.

The Baldrige Award

The Malcolm Baldrige National Quality Award is a US government/ industry venture but supported solely by the industry-funded Baldrige Award Foundation. The programme has run since 1988 and entails assessment against the criteria given in Table 6.1.

Table 6.1 Baldrige Award: points allocation by category

Category	Points
Information and analysis	60
Strategic quality analysis	90
Leadership	100
Human resource utilization	150
Quality assurance of products and services	150
Quality results	150
Customer satisfaction	300
Total	1000

Corporate developments

The increasing competitive pressure to produce higher-quality products or provide higher-quality services has brought about changes in attitudes and expectations. This is illustrated by a succession of terms used to identify acceptable goals for quality.

- *Yield* – until about 1970 the expression of quality was embodied in the term 'yield', the focus thereby being on good parts produced.
- *Scrap* – during the 1970s the focus turned to scrap as the expression highlighting the area of concern. The aim now was to reduce the waste element of a process.
- *Quality is Job 1* – by the 1980s previous levels of quality were recognized as not being competitive, so slogans such as 'Quality is Job 1' were introduced with target losses of less than 1 per cent.
- *Parts per million* – by the mid-1980s the resolve to reduce scrap still further had hardened. Phrases to convey the new aims were statements of rejects in 'parts per million' and the ideal of 'zero defects'.

Coupled with these changing attitudes and targets were a number of initiatives designed to bring about the necessary stepped improvements. These incorporated introducing (and often reintroducing) techniques together with realigning the responsibility for the achievement and control of quality as well as changing attitudes throughout an organization. Some of the key developments which illustrate the nature and extent of these changes are now described.

Statistical process control

Only through monitoring the process on a continuous basis can quality levels be systematically improved by checking the outputs from the process or system and making any necessary adjustments on an ongoing basis. This approach is known as *statistical process control* (SPC) and Figure 6.1 is an illustration of the chart used in this procedure. The way the system works is that the process average is determined and warning and action limits calculated in line with the specification. The frequency of checking is then agreed and this is undertaken by those involved, who are normally the persons responsible for making the product/providing the service. Trends are then noted and process adjustments/resetting completed where necessary.

Today many processes have an SPC-type function built into the equipment as part of the overall provision. Thus, the machine checks itself and undertakes the necessary adjustments on a continuous basis.

The overall purpose of SPC, however, is that once the process is under control (that is, products/services stay within acceptable limits) then the limits themselves are systematically reduced. In this way, companies are able to provide products/services to a higher specification and thus improve their competitive position.

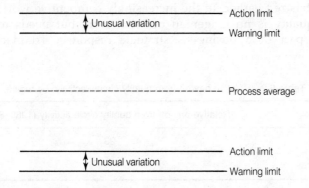

Figure 6.1 Typical control chart used in SPC procedures

Quality circles

Improving quality is achieved through a combination of better processes, better approaches/techniques and the efforts of those making the product or providing the service. The importance of the latter is best illustrated by referring to the involvement of people within the control of quality. This will be more fully addressed in the next chapter, but the use of quality circles by some organizations has made a significant contribution to this improvement.

Quality circles originated in Japan, where they were introduced as one way of improving overall performance. As many of Japanese industry's early problems had their roots in poor-quality conformance, small groups involving staff from a range of levels and disciplines were used initially to address quality problems.

By the mid-1960s several major international Japanese companies had already introduced quality circles and the effectiveness of this approach led to its widespread adoption. By the late 1980s/early 1990s an estimated 2.5 million employees were involved in quality circles in Japanese companies.

Under guidance from supervisors and middle managers, a quality circle (usually comprising 5–20 employees) chooses a problem related to quality control, productivity and similar aspects of its operation. Discussion centres on the reasons and extent of the problem and how improvements can be made.

The results of these activities are demonstrated in the quality achievements of Japanese companies and have been reported widely.[1] However, research[2] indicates that the relative pay-off from quality circles varies from region to region, as shown in Table 6.2.

Total quality management

As emphasized earlier, in the increasingly competitive world of the 1990s, quality is no longer an optional extra but needs to be an integral part of a business's strategic response. To meet these

Table 6.2   Relative pay-off from quality circles activity, by region

Region	Relative pay-off from quality circle activity (1988–89)
Europe	23
Japan	3
US	12

Note: A low number indicates a high rate of pay-off.

requirements demands total commitment from the entire organization. One approach which has been developed to highlight the need and to provide the direction necessary to achieve these goals is that of *total quality management* (TQM).

The 1980s witnessed a rapid growth in the emphasis upon quality. Data on customer preferences in 1986 indicated that eight out of ten buyers within international, industrial and consumer markets made quality equal to, or more important than, price in their purchase value decisions. This represented an increase of over 50 per cent on a similar survey conducted in 1979.[3] This change has had a major, and often volatile, influence on the business results of organizations, a factor which led to a recognition of the need to develop it as an integral part of a business. One part of this response has been TQM, the essential precepts of which are outlined below:

1. Quality is neither a technical function nor a department but a systematic process extending through an organization.

2. Quality is the concern of everyone and must be correctly structured within an organization to create these conditions.

3. The emphasis on quality must take place through all phases of the business and not just in the operations process.

4. Quality achievement must be driven externally (by the customer) and not internally (by the company).

5. Quality provision needs to be supported by appropriate new technology from computer-aided design to computer-aided quality measurement and control.

6. Achieving widespread quality improvement needs to be based on the participation and contribution of those responsible for completing the task and not a group of specialists.

7. Organizations need to have a clear, customer-orientated quality management system where the understanding, ownership and development is vested in all concerned.

When introducing TQM, the following seven steps should be followed:[4]

1. *Leadership.* The first step to achieving quality excellence is the decision to make quality leadership a fundamental strategic goal. Unless this is forthcoming the financial resources and management commitment will not be made.

2. *Company-wide introduction.* The essence of TQM is conveyed in the phrase itself. Company-wide commitment is an integral part of the approach and the company-wide introduction of TQM is an essential feature of its successful adoption.

3. *Corporate orientation.* Moving towards TQM involves reorientating a number of approaches including continuous improvement in quality levels, process control and structures and systems to provide essential support.

4. *Motivation, education and training.* To achieve continuous improvement in quality levels requires a high motivation of those involved together with the knowledge base necessary to undertake the tasks on hand. Companies need, therefore, to provide education and training relevant to the tasks to be undertaken.

5. *The robust function.* An essential feature of achieving high and constant levels of quality is building quality into the product/service at the design stage.[5]

6. *Cost orientation.* The objectives underpinning customer choice are achieved through optimizing both product/service design and process/delivery system development in line with quality and cost, and using the quality (or Taguchi) loss function to quantify quality improvements both in terms of cost and for use in agreeing tolerance bands.[6] This function alters the perspective of the best way to measure quality by linking it to a cost base.

7. *Customer orientation.* The final step is to apply quality control principles to design, thereby formulating a mechanism for ensuring that customer requirements are incorporated into the design and development phases of provision.

Service issues

The recognition that different dimensions relate to different markets has been one factor which has reinforced the need to address other criteria which relate to markets. In service organizations quality is increasingly highlighted as one such factor, and yet some inherent difficulties bring problems regarding its provision. These include the following:

1. the intangible nature of services, which involves dealing with something which people deliver to other people;

2. setting standards needs to take into account both the provider's and customer's perception of quality;

3. controlling quality during the process has to avoid interfering with service provision.

To overcome these inherent difficulties is an essential part of the operations function's role and recognizing and addressing the following will help in that regard.

Determining the facets of the service package

A service comprises four distinct facets. Separating out these different parts will help check specifications, set standards and ensure control takes place.

1. Supporting facilities – these comprise the physical resources which must be in place before a service can be offered. Features to be determined include exterior design, interior appointment, layout and supporting equipment.

2. Facilitating goods – concerns the materials and goods purchased or consumed as part of the service and to be assessed on the grounds of quality, quantity and choice.

3. Explicit services – refers to the perceivable benefits which comprise the essential feature of the service, assessed on factors such as availability, consistency of provision and the range of choice on offer.

4. Implicit services – these comprise the psychological benefits which a customer may perceive or experience and which are ancillary to the service itself (for example, punctuality, level of privacy and trouble-free nature of the provision). Relevant features relating to this include server attitudes, atmosphere and convenience of entering the service delivery system.

By separating the service package into these four elements and then reviewing the factors comprising each element, organizations are better able to recognize what comprises the service, the current level of provision and to identify which aspects to improve.

When undertaking this review, additional insights are provided by using the following perspectives:

1. assessing the back-room/front-office mix and identifying any parts of the service which may be moved from one to the other;

2. the position of each facet of the service package (as detailed in the last section) within the service delivery system;
3. the existing points of customer contact, assessing the essential provision and identifying how well it is currently being provided.

Part of the review will be to assess levels of current provision and part will be to identify opportunities to improve current provision by changing the service specification and/or the points of delivery or task completion.

Key points review

The raised profile of quality is one of the more significant changes in the business world during recent years. To understand the issues involved requires a clear understanding of the facets of quality, the relevance of each and approaches to follow to provide these options. This chapter has aimed to cover these aspects and the key points are now reviewed:

1. *Conformance quality.* This chapter was concerned with conformance quality – how well the production or service delivery system is able consistently to meet the given specification.

2. *Expectations of customers and consumers have increased.* To meet these, national and corporate developments have been introduced. The principal ones referred to in the chapter are
   (a) national developments:
      (i) BS 5750/ISO 9000 – certification procedures covering all aspects of quality;
      (ii) The Baldrige Award;
   (b) corporate developments:
      (i) changing corporate goals with new aims in terms of 'parts per million' and 'zero defects';
      (ii) statistical process control (SPC);
      (iii) quality circles;
      (iv) Total Quality Management (TQM).

3. *The facets of a service.* Identifying these and establishing the necessary specification for each are key factors in achieving the quality requirements of a service.

Notes

1. For example, 'Why does Britain want quality circles', *Production Engineering* (February 1980), pp. 45–6; J. D. Blair and J. V. Hurwitz, 'Quality circles for American firms? some unanswered questions and their implications for managers', in J. M. Lee and G. Schwendiman (eds.), *Management by Japanese Systems*, Praeger, New York, 1983; and D. L. Dewar, *The Quality Circle Guide to Participation Management*, Prentice Hall, Englewood Cliffs, NJ, 1982.
2. 'Beyond the Quality Revolution: US Manufacturing Strategy in the 1990s: Executive Summary of the 1990 Manufacturing Futures Survey' Manufacturing Round Table, School of Management, Boston University, Mass.
3. A. V. Feigenbaum, 'Total quality developments in the 1990s: an international perspective', in R. L. Chase (ed.), *Total Quality Management*, IFS/Springer-Verlag, Bedford, 1988, p. 3.
4. Based on L. P. Sullivan, 'The seven stages in company-wide quality control', in Chase, op. cit., pp. 11–19.
5. For example, refer to G. Taguchi, *Designing Quality into Products and Processes*, Asian Productivity Organisation, 1986.
6. Ibid.

7

The job of work in the 1990s

The shape of organizations and the roles of staff within them are constantly changing in order to reflect the needs of markets and the organizational responses developed to meet these needs. The 1980s witnessed a reversal in terms of attitudes and approaches to organizational responsibilities and structures which is proving to be only the prelude to a major shift in the way in which companies manage their business and get things done.

To explain this it is necessary to spell out some of the basics. The early sections of this chapter, therefore, review some of the past developments in redefining work and also outline the current philosophies underpinning organizational structures and the distribution of responsibilities. The remainder of the chapter then discusses the necessary changes which most companies need to undertake if they are to succeed in the competitive environment of the 1990s.

Managerial philosophies of work

Companies have developed organizational structures since the 1950s on a number of principles and the key ones are outlined below.

The use of specialists

Most Western firms make extensive use of specialists to run their businesses. Companies create functions involving specialist staff who supply expert advice, guidance and activity in their selected areas. The intention is to provide major line functions with the necessary help in terms of infrastructure provision within the organization. In the last four or five decades control through specialisms has been a growing feature in most organizations.

Economies of scale

The rationale for bringing together staff to provide a high level of specialist support and to help line functions to meet the needs of the business is based on the principle of economies of scale. This basic principle, however, underpins many other aspects of current business philosophy – for example, the argument for single sites and the aim of utilizing capacity to the full.

Control to the nth degree

Many organizations aim to exercise control in the greatest of detail. In the wake of this has come detailed analysis of workplace routines, procedures, systems and controls which have been purposefully specified to a low level within the organization.

In many firms this philosophy has been used indiscriminately and has directly contributed to the growing size of specialist functions, and to essential tasks being completed by the wrong part of the organization.

Control from a distance

Procedures and controls have too often been developed and installed from a distance. The specialists involved have approached their tasks with an analytical detachment in terms of the function or business concerned, with the solutions based upon some theoretical view of what should ideally take place rather than developing the controls and procedures around what really happens. Furthermore, the maintenance and development of these is not far-reaching enough and often too late. The result is that the controls and procedures often fall into disuse rather than being withdrawn or modified to meet changing needs.

Outcomes

The rationale underpinning the concept of control by specialists is to bring together staff to provide a level of capability, support and development to help line functions meet the needs of a business. Underpinned by the principle of economies of scale, the placement of these jobs within an organization has traditionally been on a functional basis and in a reporting structure outside the main line functions. The outcome is that these arrangements are proving ineffective for a number of reasons.

1. *The question of ownership* – the lack of understanding between line and staff functions is legendary. In recent years words such as 'user-orientated' have come to form part of an attempt to overcome the inherent difficulties of this organizational arrangement.

2. *Role clarity* – the roles and relationships shared by line and staff functions within the common decision procedures in which they are involved have led, in certain instances, to a large measure of misunderstanding and criticism. This is due, in part, to the people themselves, the different salary, reporting and working structures involved, the implied criticism of specialist activity, the high level of failures and apparent lack of interest or time allocation by specialists in the post-implementation period. Line managers invariably see the specialist function as a means of improving an area of operational weakness. As busy executives, there is a tendency for line managers to take a reactive role in the key periods of the development programme. The results are far from effective.

3. *Organizational relevance* – the principle of control through specialisms and economies of scale is appropriate where markets are high-volume and stable in nature. The 1980s saw markets increasingly moving away from these characteristics and this trend is continuing in the 1990s. It is essential, therefore, that companies reconsider the way they organize in order to identify ways in which relevance can be improved.

4. *Functional silos* – in many organizations, the growing areas of responsibility attributed to specialists have led to the development of independent reporting structures. This means that key sets of responsibilities which need to be integrated are now

separated. The outcome is that functional silos have evolved in which individual goals and objectives, rather than support of a line function's activities, tend to be the higher priority.

5. *Control from a distance* – one result of controlling through specialisms has been the growing tendency to believe that effective management can be maintained at a distance, using controls, systems and feedback which have been developed by specialists. This has led to situations where the hands-off controls have been insufficient to reflect key trends and those responsible for monitoring control have lacked the knowledge and experience to detect adverse trends and ask essential questions.

6. *Too many layers* – one consequence of this approach is that companies evolve into organizations with too many layers of management. The increased complexity is typically resolved by designing complex systems and structures. This adds more complexity and orientates management attention to system defects and improvements rather than the effectiveness of the structure itself.

Traditional approaches

One major outcome of the organizational structures which result from the managerial philosophies towards work discussed above has been the impact on the job of work for those engaged physically in making the product or providing the service. The result has typically been a narrowing of responsibility and deskilling of the task. Companies have employed a number of approaches to address this problem, and the more commonly used ones are now outlined.

Job enlargement

Job enlargement increases the scope of the job by adding to the number of operations performed. By adding to the horizontal nature of the job it increases the variety of the work to be completed and skills to be used and, where possible, provides a programme of work which constitutes an identifiable, whole task.

Job rotation

Sometimes it is not possible to enlarge jobs as a way of increasing their intrinsic interest. Also, in many service organizations, certain jobs have to be performed throughout the normal day or on a twenty-four-hour basis – for example, the check-out counter in a library or supermarket, and the night shift in fire, police and hospital services. In the first example, the task is monotonous but does not lend itself to enlargement. In the second, although the tasks and responsibilities are often of a higher order, the unsocial nature of the shift patterns involved makes it undesirable to most people.

Job enrichment

Whereas job enlargement widens the scope of the job, job enrichment also increases the job depth giving people a greater responsibility to organize and control the work which has to be done. For these changes to be effective the climate within an organization has to be developed as well as the necessary information on which to base sensible decisions. In the early stages, at least, many within the organization will view job enrichment as including a measure of role reversal and an erosion of their own set of responsibilities.

Changing work schedules

In a society that increasingly debates the need for a reduced working week, certain part-step developments are being made as a way forward. The first of these is a working week comprising the normal weekly hours but worked over four days to allow a longer weekend period. The second is the introduction of flexitime, which allows employees a certain amount of freedom in selecting working hours. The basis for a flexitime arrangement is that each person is required to be at work during certain 'core' hours but otherwise can choose, within certain procedural agreements, the pattern of working for a particular day or week.[1]

Participation

Employee participation in the decisions and developments within the business can be at varying levels and degrees of formality. The hallmark of a participative management style is the recognition of the valuable contribution which employees can make in many aspects of the business. At one end of the scale, employees' advice is sought on job-related issues (including job design) and at each stage in the decision-making process. At the other end of the scale, forms of industrial democracy have been developed which place worker representatives in all organizational decision-making bodies, including the board of directors.[2]

In recent years, employers have increasingly been urged to take action to improve employee communication and involvement. Under the Employment Act 1982, UK employers are required to detail in annual company reports the progress being made on employee participation. Some argue that the requirement for industrial democracy should be taken further, with a statutory framework for industrial democracy in the UK based on the EEC Fifth and Vredeling Directives. On the other hand, many believe that legally imposed structures will not work in practice.

Whatever stance is taken, the move towards participation is gaining momentum. Whether stimulated by demonstrated corporate improvement, responding to the changes in society or reflecting the felt need of many operations managers, changes are taking place. The most practical counter-argument to improvement through legislation is to demonstrate intent. One important factor, however, in establishing and developing realistic and workable improvements in participation is to give the authority for this activity to those who have responsibility for it – operations managers.[3]

For this responsibility to be reorientated to the production/ operations function, an alternative set of views needs to be held and put forward by the managers charged with the responsibility for managing the people involved. In the past, in both manufacturing and service industries, operations management has delegated the responsibility for its initiatives. The outcome has been a whole series of answers which have left the problem unresolved.[4] After years of initiatives and endeavours, many organizations still do not have a committed and motivated workforce. This lies partly with the approach: specialists observe and prescribe from a distance, and their perspective is often too narrow and certainly lacks the essential touch with reality. To be successful in managing people a manager needs to start by liking them and knowing that there is real talent which has to be tapped.[5] For this reason and the pragmatic need to place the responsibility for developing this critical resource with those with executive authority, operations management has to spearhead developments to meet current and future needs.

Operations management alternatives

For many companies, the current organizational structures consisting of line and support functions are proving less than effective. Based on organizational developments to meet the needs of stable and high-volume markets, current businesses are finding that these structures are no longer meeting their needs. These principles increasingly fail to meet today's markets which are characterized by low volumes and instability set in an environment of increasing competition, world-wide overcapacity and dynamic markets.

Any evaluation of structures and detailed roles, however, needs to be based on the question whether they will meet the requirements of the business. If firms are to compete effectively in world markets then their structures need to be both dynamic and designed to tap the relative potential of all their employees. The suggested changes which follow question whether the existing responsibility structures reflect today's requirements and highlight areas where all within the business can more easily make a full and appropriate contribution within the business.

Before addressing some of the alternative approaches which businesses need to consider, it would be worthwhile to recognize some of the more fundamental changes of a strategic and tactical nature which have been and are taking place in all organizations.

Many businesses have developed with too little forethought and too little cohesion regarding the product/service range offered, the plant/facility to provide them and how they compete in the market. This has partly been because of incremental growth and the failure to address the question of what are the key requirements for businesses to be successful. It is important when dealing with the job of work to recognize that the overall task for a plant or service facility is determined at the strategic level. How this task is then completed is partly strategic and partly tactical.

The principal perspective underlying these strategic considerations is that of facilities focus.[6] This necessitates that businesses concern themselves with identifying how they compete in the marketplace, recognizing that the issues to be addressed involve the effectiveness of the whole organization and not just of the operators, processes and systems used. The concept is to focus each facility on a limited set of products/services that are compatible with each other in terms of the operation function's task involved and the support functions required and then harness the process/service system and operational infrastructure to focus on a set of explicit tasks to meet identified market needs.[7] By doing this, organizations set the parameters of the task and support requirements. This enables them to measure the work patterns, structure and responsibilities against these clearly defined parameters, thereby ensuring that what is decided at both the strategic and tactical levels is completed against a common set of criteria which, in turn, reflect the organizational task to be successful in the marketplace.

Turning now to tactical issues, the responsibility for achieving corporate objectives lies with those responsible for the main functions in a business. The operations management role is large and complex, and nowhere more so than in the people-at-work aspects of this task. It is essential, therefore, that the operations manager thinks through the various work structures available to ensure the ideas reflect the practical issues involved and the reality of the work situation. Some important perspectives are now identified regarding this role.

- In order to continue the productivity gains essential to improving living standards, the 'doing' part of work will continue to be deskilled and simplified. Whether this reduces fatigue, boredom or skill is not important in terms of stimulating or justifying the change. Such changes are a prerequisite to productivity improvement. For many people, work is synonymous with the manual task. But work is more than this: it also involves planning, organizing, controlling and monitoring activities. Therefore, the way to increase job interest in the future will be principally through the non-manual aspects of work.

- It is important to move away from descriptions of *jobs* to descriptions of *work*. Where there is an increasing need to be flexible in both the short and longer term, detailed descriptions at the job level may offer improved control at a particular moment in time but be a source of inflexibility and unnecessary cost thereafter. It is important to avoid job descriptions by defining objectives to be achieved by groups, sections or departments. Although this is superficially less efficient, it provides a better environment in which ideas and improvements can be generated from the essential activity of the business and encourages a flexible response to the changing requirements of the organization (see Figure 7.1).

- With increases in volume and the move towards functional specialisms and line assembly, the engineering view of

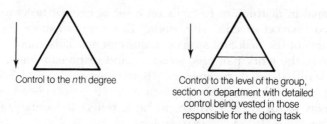

Source: Terry Hill, *Production/Operations Management: Text and cases* (2nd edn), Prentice Hall International: Hemel Hempstead, 1991, p. 445 (with permission).

Figure 7.1   Changes in the concept of control

orderliness is segregated tasks and straight lines. Thus, the enlargement of work is difficult. It is essential, therefore, that configurations of work avoid both the unnecessary breakdown and separation of tasks and the layout of work using straight lines (see Figure 7.2).

• The rationale for employing specialists is not only to bring in expertise but also to provide support to the line. Figure 7.3 illustrates what tends to happen in many organizations with the introduction of specialist functions. Over time, the gap between specialists and a line may widen because of their geographical separation within the plant, the value system under which they both judge the other, and the pursuit of different personal and organizational objectives. For these reasons the ownership of problems and their solutions, controls, procedures and systems tend to be seen in departmental rather than corporate terms.

An important role of operations managers is to develop the areas for which they are responsible. Given the high levels of investment expenditure that fall within the function, getting it right is essential. The day-to-day pressures on the operations function at all levels and the separation of specialist inputs from the line departments tend to hinder this activity. Specialists that are put back into line functions and under the authority and responsibility of line executives will, in turn, facilitate these important improvements that will lead to greater efficiency and effectiveness. Some of the detailed changes which companies need to consider are now explained.

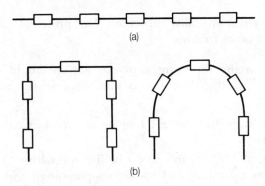

(a)

(b)

Source: Hill, op. cit., 1991, p. 446 (with permission).

Figure 7.2 The straight-line layout of alternative solutions. (a) Straight-line layout intended to meet engineering principles of process design. (b) The same work, the revised layout of which facilitates communication and work identity

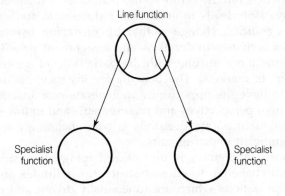

Line function

Specialist function

Specialist function

Source: Hill, op. cit., 1991, p. 439 (with permission).

Figure 7.3 The separation of activities from existing line functions to more recently created specialist functions

Functional teamwork concept

As stressed earlier, a fundamental change which Western companies need to consider is the breakdown of the currently held view of line and support functions. The alternative is to consider a move to build specialist functions back into the line and for them to report within that authority/responsibility structure. The principal consequences of this would be as follows:

1. changes in the reporting structure, which would remove the problem of the line management/specialist interface not working;

2. clarification of the current role of specialists into those areas which are

    (a) primarily within the scope of the specialism (for example, quality assurance and operations planning); and
    (b) those which should be under the auspices of the line management function (for example, quality control, continuous improvement activities and production control).

This enables an organization, therefore, to build its structure around sets of coherent, interrelated activities rather than, as at present, around activities which have similar names. Pushing decision-making activity from the centre to the plant and from specialists into the line invariably leads to an overall reduction in staff. However, the most significant change is that by reshaping overheads, the relevance of activities undertaken and assignment priorities established become more in tune with the basic tasks of a business and support for its markets. The benefit, for instance, for operations managers to have the opportunity to generate cost analyses in line with their own perspectives and requirements and in line with their contribution to corporate decisions is overwhelmingly logical and leads to significant improvements.

The process, therefore, is one of reshaping overheads. It is a fundamental challenge to current structures, attitudes and expectations. Organizations which are functionally driven and controlled through specialisms are top-heavy and unresponsive, and fail to use the ability of their people and the opportunity of their investments. Built into this new approach is the rationale for continuous improvement which results in becoming not only more cost-efficient but also more strategically effective.

The structure of work

The realization that work constitutes more than the 'doing' tasks is at the root of change in the structure of work. As illustrated in Figure 7.4 work comprises planning, doing and evaluating.

With the approach to organizational structure based on specialisms, work other than strict 'doing' tasks has been allocated to

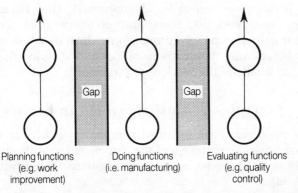

Planning functions　　Doing functions　　Evaluating functions
(e.g. work　　(i.e. manufacturing)　　(e.g. quality
improvement)　　　　control)

Source: Terry Hill, *Manufacturing Strategy: The strategic management of the manufacturing function* (2nd edn), Macmillan, Basingstoke, 1993, p. 231 (with permission).

Figure 7.4　The elements of work and the gap between them created by the organizational structure

support functions which report in separate systems. Figure 7.5 suggests how parts of those planning and evaluating activities should be reassigned to those currently responsible for doing the tasks.

In this way such an action not only lends support to the arguments of building specialists back into the line but also provides a tangible, common-sense illustration of the effect this can have. These actions facilitate continuous improvement activities while

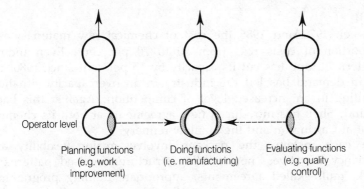

Operator level

Planning functions　　Doing functions　　Evaluating functions
(e.g. work　　(i.e. manufacturing)　　(e.g. quality
improvement)　　　　control)

Source: Hill, op. cit., 1993, p. 234 (with permission).

Figure 7.5　The doing task which now incorporates appropriate planning and evaluating steps, so much an intrinsic part of work

creating greater job interest for all concerned. They release specialists from 'non-specialist' work and give operators work which involves the three important dimensions which make up meaningful tasks by broadening their responsibilities and allowing them both to plan and to evaluate the work they carry out.

Examples to illustrate what can happen

There is an increasing number of companies which are rethinking the organizational structure and the responsibility/authority relationships within them. Some examples to illustrate what can happen are now provided.

DuPont

Before DuPont's Maitland plant made structural changes within operations, a customer's quality complaint was handled by head office. Now the operator who made the product visits the customer and decides how to correct the problem. Problems are cleared up more quickly and customers are happier. At the other end of the spectrum,

> staring at a bank of computers is not a stimulating way to spend a 12-hour shift. To make [the operators'] job more interesting and more useful to the company, [they] are trained – in their off-hours and at overtime rates – in computer technology. They then become responsible for maintaining computers in the plant's control room and for helping to develop expert systems.[8]

Shell

Between 1972 and 1985 the cost of chemical raw materials as a proportion of costs rose from 50 to 70 per cent. Even though Western Europe has cut its capacity by 15 per cent since 1980, the fall in demand has left the industry in an overcapacity situation, resulting in an increased level of competition. Against this background, Shell has introduced new agreements at both its chemical plant at Carrington and the Stanlow refinery.

In each instance the package involves major flexibility and efficiency initiatives, new grading structures, revised patterns of work, multi-skilled agreements, appropriate training programmes and revised manning agreements. Shell has recognized the need to manage people in a way that provides an opportunity to increase their contribution in meeting the requirements of the business.

At the Carrington chemical plant, the heart of the agreement concerns changes in working practice, the concept of multi-skilled technicians and a common union approach. From 1985, six teams of technicians complete any operating and maintenance work with support from two service groups and outside contractors. Other features of the development include new grading structures, revised shift patterns, training programmes and remuneration agreements (including redeployment assistance).

At the Stanlow refinery, the core of the agreement concerns flexibility agreements for craft and non-craft employees and their implications for grading structures, shift patterns and union representation. In addition, short, disruptive daily breaks have been replaced by five additional days' annual holiday, appropriate training programmes introduced and changes in total remuneration concerning career progression, grading structures and redundancy/redeployment packages.[9]

Digital Equipment Corporation (DEC)

In mid-1986, DEC, faced with the prospect of a decline in business, recognized the need to introduce product changes and to adopt a strategic response within the business in terms of c~ ng with the required technical change and resultant flexibility. G..v n the short life cycle nature of its products, the company need 1 not only processes that could cope with changing product specifications but also a workforce that could respond appropriately. For th t reason it introduced at its plant in Ayr autonomous work-groups of some twelve people who had 'front-to-back' responsibility for the product in order to create the necessary flexibility within each group. The company moved to a skill-based payment system[10] which rewards people for the skills they have rather than the job they do, thereby promoting the necessary flexibility within the group working arrangements. In addition, it moved several support activities (such as material acquisition and production control) to the shop floor. Further ways of increasing shop-floor involvement included improved features of communication, product ownership by the groups and appropriate training.[11]

Komatsu

Commercial pressures facing Komatsu, the Japanese construction equipment company, have forced it to set up offshore manufacturing facilities to enable it to respond more closely to particular market needs whilst avoiding trade friction and reducing the impact of fluctuating currency rates. After setting up factories in Brazil, Mexico, Indonesia and the USA, Komatsu set up its European facility in Birtley, Gateshead, in mid-1987. Flexibility and teamwork were considered to be essential to meeting its market demands and these factors are, therefore, strongly in evidence in its agreements. These agreements relate to all full-time staff up to and including the supervisors.[12] They contain procedures for avoiding disputes, flexibility and the use of manpower and single-status employment conditions, with a common pension scheme, performance review, career appraisal, sick-pay arrangements, monthly pay, free medical cover and a 39-hour week with five weeks' holiday.

Other applications
There are many other examples in the UK and elsewhere which illustrate this growing trend. In the UK they include Trebor, Borgwarner, Rowntree Mackintosh, Balfour Beatty Northern Construction Division, Blue Circle and the Austin Rover Group.[13] In the USA they include Shenandoah Life Insurance, Cummins Engines, General Motors, Procter and Gamble, Tektronix and other DEC businesses.

Cascading overheads

Linked to both the structure of work and the role of specialists within an organization, companies should seek to push work as far down the organization as possible. Coupled to an investment by the firm in the training of the individuals involved, the systematic cascading of overheads will help to increase the level of flexibility required, allow any spare time created as a by-product of process investments to be usefully absorbed whilst also providing those involved with a more meaningful task. This involves changing the levels at which decisions are made and allowing people to decide on how best to complete tasks once they have been given the relevant parameters and information involved. As Figure 7.1 illustrates, it changes the concept of control from one which controls to the nth degree to one where the control is placed at the appropriate level in the organization.

Quality circles or quality improvement groups

As part of the organizational changes advocated here, the introduction of quality circles or productivity improvement groups needs careful consideration. Before such an introduction it is important that companies carefully evaluate their role and contribution, a factor which has not always been exercised by Western companies. In many instances they have been perceived as panaceas and as such have been evaluated and implemented at an operational level and not as part of a strategic organizational change. This essential difference in the way the quality circles are perceived goes some way to explaining the overall rating attributed to this activity and reported in the 1990 *Manufacturing Futures Survey*[14] and previously given in Table 6.2. This assesses the level of pay-off over the two-year period, 1988–9, compared with the other 26 activities listed in the survey.

The concept of quality circles emanates from Japanese business practice. It illustrates the impact of participation on the productivity increases which can be achieved in all aspects of performance by systematically involving workers in the improvement of quality, productivity and similar operations activities.

The failure of Western manufacturing companies to recognize the value of the shop floor's contribution is widespread. The use of quality circles or productivity improvement groups, however, is an aid to redressing this imbalance and 'tapping what is probably our most underdeveloped asset – the gold in the mind of our workers'.[15] For this to be effective, however, the company needs to be genuinely committed to the principle of continuous improvement and to accept that this can only be achieved by top management's participation. In this way, companies are able to start tapping into their collective wisdom. The change, however, is a strategic one. It accepts that there are significant benefits to be derived from detailed operational improvements, implemented quickly and effectively on a participative basis, and that people, as a group, have the ability to evaluate each other's ideas and developments.

Participative management, however, is not a soft style. It is both demanding and results-orientated. The differences are embodied in the changed views of work and relative contribution of those involved. Functions, and groups of people who are potential contributors, need to be clearly identified. Similarly, other functions and groups need to be placed in their relative positions on the continuum depicting these features in terms of the business's needs. Fulfilling potential or eliminating low contributors will bring noticeable improvements.

Empowering people
Most of what the forgoing has been addressing is captured under the term 'empowering people'. Using this or derivatives of the

phrase such as 'empowered organizations' and 'empowered partnerships', companies aim to signal the way in which they wish to proceed based on levels of involvement which are of an order of magnitude greater than the traditional forms of the past described in an earlier section of this chapter on 'traditional approaches'. Empowering people is recognized as an essential way to achieve significant and lasting improvements. However, although the logic is indisputable and the benefits clearly identifiable, getting there is another issue. There are many important perspectives and potential difficulties which need to be recognized, the more important of which are described here.

Issues and problems

- It is essential for companies to bear in mind that empowering people needs to be an evolutionary process. Making bold statements that everyone is now 'empowered' or attempting changes of a stepped nature will not work. Training, reorientation, and introducing changes in procedures and reporting structures need to be implemented with realistic time-scales.

- It will invariably be more difficult for specialists/managers to cope with these changes as they are 'giving away' responsibilities, tasks and status. The recipients of the change will also experience their own sets of problems but, overall, 'receiving' will tend to be easier to cope with than 'giving'.

- Companies must ensure that the reward systems do not get in the way. Creating ambivalent situations where job/development activities conflict with monetary rewards must be avoided.

- Organizations will need to recognize and cope with 'obsolete' managers and specialists. When changes like these are made, many existing functions will no longer be required and existing attitudes to change and what constitutes career progression will be turned inside out.

- Where corporations are introducing these changes, it will be easier to manage and develop these first-time applications on a small independent site or in a less critical part of the total business. Once some learning has taken place, these ideas will be more readily accepted in main sites and critical areas of the business.

- Creating the will in those involved is a key element of these changes.

- Executives need to have realistic lead-time expectations for all phases of this change programme. Allocating insufficient calendar time will undermine the success of these developments.

- Changes of this magnitude will bring about difficulties and mistakes will happen. Expectations and supporting ways of dealing with problems as they arise must be well thought through in advance. If not, there will be a tendency for management to overcontrol these developments.

- One of management's key roles is to facilitate change. Reshaping information systems and realigning other functions' expectations are essential parts of their role.

- Specialists often find great difficulty in passing on technical information in a non-threatening manner. The difficulties arise from an inherent inability to communicate in a receptive way and an overriding fear in some that undertaking these tasks will lead to a distinct possibility of working themselves out of a job.

Changing roles
It is important to recognize that the roles of all will change. Operators and staff will have increased responsibility which includes undertaking non-doing tasks; specialists will need to become consultants; and managers will take on the key role of facilitators.

Key points review

Change is at the very root of business. Markets, products and process technologies are continuously evolving and changes can often be of a stepped nature. It is essential, therefore, for the organization to reflect these in the way it manages and controls its functions. Within the operations function one critical area of development is that of people and their role within the support of markets. This chapter has addressed these developments, and the key points are now listed.

1. *Managerial philosophies* to work have evolved since the 1950s which currently form the basis on which many organizations are built. However, these perspectives are increasingly being challenged or recognized as being less than appropriate to today's demanding times.

2. *Traditional approaches* to work, however, have comprised simple refinements to classic views of work and approaches to its management and control.

3. *Operations management alternatives* are required which fundamentally change the way in which work and its management and control are perceived. The principal ones (together with some examples) were then discussed in the latter part of the chapter:

   (a) functional teamwork concept;
   (b) cascading overheads;
   (c) quality circles or productivity improvement groups.

   The nature of the change is captured in the phrase 'empowerment of people' and signals a fundamental way in which companies are organized.

Notes

---

1. For further details on flexitime refer to P. J. Sloane, *Changing Patterns of Working Hours*, Department of Employment, Manpower Paper No. 13, HMSO, London, 1975; E. S. Drye, 'Flexible Hours in DHSS local offices', *Management Services in Government* (February 1975); and T. Burt, 'Making the most of time with flexible working hours', *Personnel Executive* (March 1982), pp. 37–45.

2. For a discussion on some of these developments refer to R. Harrison, *Workers Participation in Western Europe*, IPM, London, 1976; J. Crisp, *Industrial Democracy in Western Europe: a North American perspective*, McGraw-Hill Ryerson Ltd, New York, 1978; J. Hebden and J. Shaw, *Pathways to Participation*, Associated Business Programmes, London, 1977; D. Guest and K. Knight (eds), *Putting Participation into Practice*, Gower, Aldershot, 1977; and Geursten Report, European Parliament Working Document 1-862/81 (15 January 1982) concerning employee participation.

   In addition, specific applications of participation described in individual organizations provide important insights into these developments. See, for example, V. Kiam, 'Remington's marketing and manufacturing strategies', *Management Review* (February 1987) pp. 43–55.

3. Peter Wilkins, *The Road to Nissan: Flexibility, quality, teamwork*, Macmillan, Basingstoke, 1987; highlights the need to give back to the production function the responsibility for managing this part of the business.

4. Some of these issues are neatly summarized by Wickham Skinner, 'Big hat, no cattle: managing human resources', *Harvard Business Review* (September/October 1981), pp. 106–14.

5. One illustration of different attitudes to the role of people is provided by K. Matsushita, 'Why the West will lose', *Industrial Participation* (Spring 1988), p. 8, a paper based on extracts of remarks made by him to a group of Western managers.

6. The concept of focus was first introduced by Wickham Skinner, 'The Focused Factory', *Harvard Business Review* (May/June 1974), pp. 113–31. It is more fully addressed in Terry Hill, *Manufacturing Strategy: Text and cases*, Irwin, Homewood, Ill., pp. 98–112; and Terry Hill, *Manufacturing Strategy: The strategic management of the manufacturing function* (2nd edn), Macmillan, Basingstoke, 1993, pp. 156–83.

7. See Hill, op. cit., 1993, pp. 157–8.

8. A detailed review of the changes at DuPont's Maitland Plant is given in D. Stoffman, 'Less is More', Report on *Business Magazine* (June 1988), pp. 90–101.

9. A more detailed account of these agreements is provided in Industrial Relations Review and Report (IR-RR) 358 (17 December 1985) published by Industrial Relations Services, 67 Maygrove Road, London NW6 2EJ.

10. For details on skill-based payment systems see Terry Hill, *Production/ Operations Management: Text and cases* (2nd edn), Prentice Hall International, Hemel Hempstead, 1991, Chapter 15.

11. An account of the DEC approach is given in David Buchanan, 'Job enrichment is dead: long live high-performance work design 1', *Personnel Management* (May 1987), pp. 40–3.

12. Further details of this agreement are given in IR-RR 391 (5 May 1987) published by Industrial Relations Services.

13. Details of the applications of Rowntree Mackintosh, Balfour Beatty Northern Construction Division and Blue Circle are provided in IR-RR 349, 360 and 366, respectively, published by Industrial Relations Services.

14. *Manufacturing Futures Survey* (1990), INSEAD, Fontainbleau, France.

15. J. R. Ambrose, 'Quality Control Circles: the West adopts a Japanese concept', *International Management* (December 1980), p. 31.

Index